Advance Praise for Helping Groups Heal

"This book is full of practical counseling skills, relevant Biblical insights, down-to-earth examples, and other helpful tools for use with groups. I am enthusiastic in my recommendation of this well-written book."
—Gary R. Collins, PhD, author of *Christian Counseling*, *Christian Coaching* and *How to Be a People Helper*

"What an ideal team to write a book! Jan Hook is a wise and experienced practitioner with hundreds of groups under his belt, and Joshua Hook and Don Davis are exceptional clinical and basic researchers who also have a wealth of experience in group treatments. The result is *Helping Groups Heal: Leading Small Groups in the Process of Transformation*, which is a must-read book for Christian small group leaders who want to help the people in those groups grow and heal. Experienced group leader or rookie, this is a book that can enrich you and your group participants."
—Everett L. Worthington, Jr., author of *The Power of Forgiving* and *Humility: The Quiet Virtue*

"*Helping Groups Heal* is a must-read book. The authors have written a fantastic resource that should be on the bookshelf of anyone serious about group work. This book will encourage and equip leaders—whether novice or experienced—to move others through a transformational process of healing and growth. Drawing on cutting-edge research, as well as years of personal and professional experience, the model laid out offers a clear, practical path for helping others experience stronger, grace-filled relationships.

— Jamie D. Aten, PhD, founder & executive director, Humanitarian Disaster Institute at Wheaton College

"Steeped in practical experience and supported by research, this gem provides insights about the potential for groups to facilitate healing and growth in their members. Written in a practical and engaging style, the team of authors provide a model of well-functioning groups which can be applied to groups ranging from formal therapy to church bible study—or anywhere in between. Whether you are the leader or participant of such a group, this book is well worth the read."

—Peter Hill, coauthor of *Psychology of Religion: An Empirical Approach*

HELPING GROUPS HEAL

Helping Groups Heal

Leading Small Groups in the Process of Transformation

Jan Paul Hook, EdD | Joshua N. Hook, PhD

Don E. Davis, PhD

TEMPLETON PRESS

Templeton Press
300 Conshohocken State Road, Suite 500
West Conshohocken, PA 19428
www.templetonpress.org

Designed and typeset by Gopa & Ted2, Inc.

Library of Congress Cataloging-in-Publication Data on file.

Printed in the United States of America

22 23 24 25   10 9 8 7 6 5 4 3 2

To Cheryl, my wife, who has always been by my side.
—Jan Paul Hook

To TM, AK, and AB: Our friendship and group meetings
helped keep me oriented toward grace.
—Joshua N. Hook

To Hal Stevens, my training director at Clemson University.
He embodied the principles of grace that are
the heart of this book.
—Don E. Davis

Contents

Acknowledgments

WRITING THIS BOOK was definitely a group effort, and I (Jan) have a huge amount of gratitude to everyone who helped me along the way. First, I want to thank my son Josh for his help throughout this process. He was the one who first encouraged me to write this book.

I also want to thank the participants in all the groups I have led over the years. From the very beginning, they have led the way, showing me how to best lead and help them. I want to thank my colleague Steven Hines, who is also one of my closest friends. We have led groups together for over twenty-five years. So much of my learning about helping groups heal has come from leading groups together with him.

I also want to thank the people who have gone before me and have been so integral in helping me to develop my thinking about the process of healing. Of course, the entire concept of healing as a function of truth and grace comes from Jesus in the Bible. I am grateful to psychologist Henry Cloud and his book *Changes That Heal*, in which he wrote about healing being a function of truth, grace, and time. I am thankful for Linda Weise, one of my colleagues at Willow Creek Community Church, who first put out the idea of healing being a cyclical process. From the idea of The Healing Cycle, I developed a training model for the leaders of the support groups at Willow Creek. I want to thank Linda for her insight, and all the leaders of the small groups that I had the pleasure to train. Their support, encouragement and feedback have been invaluable.

I am grateful to everyone at Templeton Press who helped me craft the idea of The Healing Cycle into the book you are holding today. I am especially grateful to Susan Arellano and Angelina Horst, who worked with us from beginning to end.

Finally, I want to thank my wife, Cheryl. She has always had my back.

Preface

As a counselor, I (Jan) engage with people almost every day about their deepest experiences of pain and struggle. We live in a broken world, filled with disappointment, problems, and difficulties. This is a predictable part of life. Jesus promised, "In this world you will have trouble" (John 16:33a). So this "promise" likely rings true for you. I know I have had my share of trouble in life.

I love it that the verse doesn't stop there. After noting the inevitable reality of suffering, Jesus gives us reason for hope: "But take heart! I have overcome the world" (John 16:33b). The story does not stop with brokenness and pain. Your story—and those of others you serve—doesn't have to stop there.

The overcoming life of Jesus gives us hope for healing, growth, and new life. His life and ministry demonstrate that his life is stronger than anything in this world. Sickness is terrible; Jesus healed. Physical needs are daunting; Jesus fed. Demonic possession is terrifying; Jesus set people free. Death catches up with each of us eventually; Jesus resurrected Lazarus. Clearly, this does not mean that all your troubles will go away. It did not mean that for Jesus. He was brutally killed, but then God raised him from the dead. "Take heart! I have overcome the world" is the message that echoes in fallen creation after the life of Christ.

Counselors and helpers have an opportunity to participate in this ministry of overcoming each time we interact with the people placed under our care. In my experience, of all the things that contribute to healing and growth, the most important is relationship. Brokenness occurs in relationship; *healing also happens in relationship*. That's the reason why I love small groups so much. The relationships between the small group leader and the group members are powerful, but the group members also experience the healing power of relationships *with the other group members*.

My goal in writing this book is to help group leaders be more effective in leading their small groups. Leading small groups is difficult. Some basic foundational skills can go a long way in setting up a small group that helps its members to experience life to the fullest. I have been leading small groups for the past thirty years, including several different types of small groups (e.g., therapy groups, support groups, and Bible studies). My hope for this book is that for whatever type of small group you lead, you can learn and develop skills that improve your ability to help your group members in their own process of healing and growth. Thanks for taking this journey with me.

—Jan Paul Hook

HELPING GROUPS HEAL

Introduction

L EADING SMALL GROUPS is difficult work. There is great potential for small groups to be a context for group members to experience healing and growth, but leading a small group isn't easy. To make matters worse, sometimes group leaders step into their role without much knowledge or training for how to be an effective leader. Without a baseline set of skills and tools, small group leaders often struggle.

This book is designed to help small group leaders develop basic and advanced skills to create a group context in which members can experience healing and growth. The fact that you are reading this book probably means you are already involved in running small groups. Maybe you volunteer at your church and lead a Bible study or discipleship group. Perhaps you are involved in leading support groups, such as helping people grow in their marriages, recover from a divorce, or gain freedom from an addiction. Maybe you are a mental health counselor or psychologist, leading therapy groups as part of your work. Perhaps you even are a graduate student, just beginning your training in leading groups. Whatever type of group you lead, and whatever amount of experience you have, I hope this book helps you to improve your skills in creating and maintaining a group culture that provides authentic, compassionate, and gracious relationships that bring life and growth.

This book walks through a model for group work called The Healing Cycle (Hook & Hook, 2010), which describes how small groups can promote healing and growth in six steps: grace, safety, vulnerability, truth, ownership, and repentance. First and foremost, a healing small group involves a culture of grace. In the chapter on grace, you will reflect on your own stories of brokenness, grace, and healing in order to promote a heart of grace as a leader. Out of this stance, you will learn how to offer a heart of grace to your group members.

Grace leads to the second step, safety. A culture of grace in a group allows members to feel safe with you and each other. In the chapter on safety, you will learn how to create and maintain safety in your small group. You will learn to set boundaries (e.g., setting up ground rules such as confidentiality and consistent attendance) and address boundary violations (e.g., what to do when one group member harshly criticizes another member).

Grace and safety allow for vulnerable sharing, the focus of chapter 4. Healing and growth occur in proportion to members' willingness to open up and share vulnerably. Sometimes group members stay on the surface and shrink back, because they are afraid to expose their true selves. In this chapter, you will learn techniques to promote greater vulnerability, including self-disclosure, listening, validating, and linking.

Vulnerable sharing leads to truth: group members can see themselves and their situation more clearly and honestly. In the chapter on truth, you will learn techniques to balance honesty with love so that people can see and accept the truth about themselves: their strengths and limitations. I like to call these areas for growth and change "growth edges," because it normalizes the idea that none of us is perfect—each group member has areas in their life in which they can experience healing and growth. You will also learn to teach group members similar skills in how they interact with each other and in their relationships.

Seeing themselves honestly provides group members with an opportunity for ownership, the focus of chapter 6. Ownership involves taking the right amount of responsibility for causing and maintaining one's problems. This step may involve owning that one has taken too little responsibility for a problem, or it may involve admitting that one's contribution to a problem may have been taking too much responsibility. In this way, we almost always have room to own our problems more accurately and effectively, on a strong foundation of grace, safety, vulnerability, and truth. Change rarely occurs until people own that they are in some way involved in maintaining their problems. This is not blaming the victim; this is empowering group members to accurately see what they can and cannot do, sometimes in seemingly impossible situations. This step is called "owning your truth," which includes understanding one's stories and ways these stories can be transformed. You will learn specific skills for helping group members own their truth, including teaching group members to own the stories they make up, laddering to access core stories and beliefs, working with group members' projections, confronting unhealthy patterns, and dealing with conflict.

Accurate ownership naturally leads to repentance, which is the next step in The Healing Cycle. In this chapter, you will learn how to help members repent, which involves turning away from one's problematic behaviors and walking a new path. This step is crucial to The Healing Cycle. Christians believe that they are healed from broken relational patterns through honestly acknowledging sin and brokenness and asking for forgiveness and healing. Group members carry shame from relationships and want to experience a greater sense of integrity. You will develop skills to help group members work toward healing through confession, receiving forgiveness, and commitment to behavior change and accountability.

In the final chapter, you will be introduced to the cyclical nature of The Healing Cycle. Repentance allows members to have a deep experience of grace. Instead of just head knowledge about grace, grace becomes real, as members pair ownership of their truth and awareness of personal brokenness into the grace culture of the group. Group members learn they can be fully known and loved. They do not have to hide their brokenness but can bring it into relationship with others, confess, and make lasting changes. True repentance leads to joy, as group members celebrate each other's victories and accomplishments and continue to encourage and support each other in their struggles and failures. This process repeats until people experience a growing degree of wholeness and integrity.

Let me tell you a bit about myself and my background writing this book. My name is Jan Paul Hook. The Healing Cycle is a small group model I helped develop and refine over the past twenty years. I was trained as a professional counselor at Trinity International University. After graduating, I directed the counseling center at Trinity. Running groups and supervising other counselors-in-training were central parts of my role. Next, I worked at Willow Creek Community Church, one of the first large churches to popularize small groups as an avenue for doing ministry. As a leader in their community care ministries, I trained and supervised many lay small group leaders who facilitated groups on a variety of themes, including marital restoration and divorce recovery. Currently, I am a partner in a private practice, where I lead two weekly small groups for men struggling with sexual addiction (Hook, Hook, & Hines, 2008). I train small group leaders in various settings, such as for churches and the American Association of Christian Counselors (Hook & Hook, 2015). I have also applied this model to leading Bible studies. So, in a variety of personal and professional settings, I have consistently worked on my role as a group leader.

Throughout this book, I share my own experiences from leading small groups. Many of these examples illustrate how to use the training and skills presented in this book. I give examples of dialogue that you can take and adapt to suit your needs. In addition, I share examples of times when I have struggled to implement the principles described in this book. Leading small groups can be a difficult undertaking, especially for beginning leaders, and I want to show how such struggle is common. For example, I still remember one of my first times leading a small group—a marriage group at my church—and I was excited and scared as I prepared. It was going to be different from a typical church small group because these couples really wanted to work on their marriages. I didn't want to just teach from the front of the room. I wanted the couples in the group to engage with the material and each other and apply it to their lives and marriages.

I was hopeful about the healing and growth that could occur not only in their marriages but in their families as well.

The plan for the study was to work through a book about how to have a healthy marriage. Each week we would cover a particular topic (communication, parenting, etc.), and then discuss how the topic applied to each of our marriage relationships. I was excited about the possibility for this group, but I was also nervous. Could I do this? Did I know enough about marriages to be helpful? Did I know enough about running small groups to be an effective leader? I wasn't sure, but I was going to try it anyway. I probably overprepared.

That first Sunday, the kickoff weekend of the marriage group, had been advertised at our church for several weeks. Five or six couples had expressed interest, which seemed like a fine number—not too big, not too small. I got to the church early and set up the room. Then I waited. And waited. And waited.

No one showed up. Well, one couple showed up about twenty minutes late, but that was it. It wasn't much of a group. I felt discouraged and frustrated. I tried to think about what went wrong. Maybe the day and time of the meeting were bad. Perhaps people weren't ready to commit to a group where they would have to talk about their marriage problems. Maybe the marriage group was a low priority; people might come if their marriage was on the verge of divorce, but otherwise it wasn't that big of a deal.

Maybe it was me. That thought stung the most. I wasn't some kind of fancy marriage guru. I had only been married myself for about five years and had recently finished graduate school and started working as a full-time counselor. Maybe I didn't have enough experience. Maybe I wasn't a good enough leader. A big part of me wanted to quit that first day.

One thing that kept me going was my commitment to addressing the need. I knew that folks in the church were struggling in their marriages but didn't have a place to talk about it. I knew this from talking with couples who were struggling but felt alone, like they were the only ones with a problem. My sense of calling to address this need made me confident that if I could somehow provide a context for people to give and receive help in small groups, they would experience healing and growth in their relationship and build the kind of marriage they really wanted.

So I kept going. That first day, I worked with the one couple who showed up. It wasn't much of a group—just me, my wife, and one other couple. But I kept going. I was committed to exploring the vision I had in my heart for couples at our church. Along the way, I learned a few things about doing groups—mostly by trial and error.

And then people started coming. People began supporting and helping one another in their struggles. Healing, growth, and restoration happened. The small group became a place for couples to talk about what was happening in their marriages. Couples were able to connect, support one another, seek help in parenting their children, and work through their struggles and conflicts together.

Through this experience I decided that small groups were something I wanted to focus on in my personal and professional life, so I began to lead therapy groups at my workplace and then in my private practice. For a time, I worked on the staff of a large church and trained small group leaders in a variety of different ministries, including ministries that helped distressed marriages, individuals recovering from divorce, and people struggling with addictions. Over the years, I have seen many people experience change, healing, and growth in small groups. Small groups can really work.

When I lead small groups now, I feel more at ease and confident. However, I still remember how difficult leading small groups can be, especially when you are just starting out. I am writing this book to help small group leaders who want to be good at creating groups that are safe and life-giving. I realized over time that leaders can develop certain foundational skills to help their groups run well. So much of what I had to learn through trial and error could be picked up less painfully.

In addition to my own experiences, I draw on the experiences of two coauthors. It is especially rewarding to be able to write this book with my son Josh. Josh earned his PhD in counseling psychology from Virginia Commonwealth University, and he currently works as a professor at the University of North Texas. He has published papers focused on small groups and the intersection of religion, spirituality, and counseling. He is also a licensed clinical psychologist in the state of Texas, and he teaches a multicultural counseling course that uses many of the principles of this book. Josh met Don Davis in graduate school. They worked with the same mentor and have continued to write together over the years. Don is a professor at Georgia State University, and he teaches group counseling to students training to be professional counselors. Josh and Don both have experience leading various forms of therapy groups, as well as leading and being a part of church small groups. To make it easier for the reader, the book is written from my voice, but the information presented throughout the chapters reflects our combined experiences.

WHY SMALL GROUPS?

I have devoted so much of my life and ministry to small groups because I believe they provide one of the best settings for people to experience healing and growth. As a counselor, even though I regularly refer clients to a variety of treatment modalities (e.g., individual counseling, support groups, self-help books, and church involvement), I like small groups the most.

I'm not alone. There is a long history of using groups in the counseling and psychology professions. Irvin Yalom (1970), one of the most influential figures behind the development of group therapy, was a psychiatrist who developed a group therapy focused on the interpersonal process. The main idea is that people develop problems within relationships and then perpetuate some of these interpersonal behaviors because they lack accurate feedback. They naturally bring these behaviors to group, as do others, which gives everyone a chance to work and grow. The leader's job is to help promote norms in which group members honestly but respectfully share their moment-to-moment emotional experiences with each other, based on what is happening in the group. For the first time, people have a combination of accurate feedback and emotional support to effectively use that feedback to experiment with making changes in how they relate to others. Based on his work, Yalom described eleven therapeutic factors representing the most important ways that small groups can help people change (see table 1.1). Many of these factors show up throughout the pages of this book.

Table 1: Yalom's Therapeutic Factors

THERAPEUTIC FACTOR	DESCRIPTION
Installation of hope	People often show up for small groups feeling hopeless about their situation and future. But seeing other people working and making progress can provide hope that change is possible.
Universality	When people attend a small group, they realize that they are not alone in their pain. Other people are struggling just like they are.
Imparting information	Other group members can offer helpful suggestions about a group member's problem that they haven't previously considered.
Altruism	Small groups provide a setting where group members can love and care for each other, just for the sake of doing good and being supportive.
Corrective recapitulation of the primary family group	Most families have problems, and children don't get all their needs met. In the small group, group members can have a different experience of being loved and supported, which they may have missed from their family growing up.
Development of socializing techniques	A small group allows space for group members to engage and interact with each other in a real way. If group members have problems with certain aspects of socializing, they can receive feedback and work on these issues in the group.
Imitative behavior	A small group allows members to observe other people communicate and behave. Members can learn and try to copy effective communication and behavior.

THERAPEUTIC FACTOR	DESCRIPTION
Interpersonal learning	Real relationships happen in small groups. This can be a great setting for group members to work on improving their interpersonal skills, which can then be applied outside of group.
Group cohesiveness	The single most effective predictor of people getting better in a small group is group cohesiveness. If group members feel a strong bond with each other and support each other, group members tend to experience healing and growth.
Catharsis	Small groups provide a place for group members to let out emotions. Experiencing and expressing one's emotions is important for healing and growth.
Existential factors	A small group is a place where group members can consider and discuss the big questions, such as "Why am I here?" and "What is my purpose?"

Source: Yalom (1970)

In line with Yalom's (1970) theory, I believe there are two main reasons small groups are so powerful for promoting healing and growth. First, small groups allow group members to obtain feedback and experience insight *in the moment.* Often I try to encourage group members to make a shift from talking about their problems and issues *outside the room* to exploring what they are experiencing right now *inside the room.* Counselors often refer to this shift as from content to process. We return to this point throughout the book. A core element of a healing group is a culture that involves group members engaging with each other and sharing what they are experiencing in the moment. This is the difference between learning about growth and experiencing true personal growth. When people belong to a group and make that group important to them, experiencing and applying important insights with the group, then it is only natural for them to apply this learning to their lives outside the group.

A second reason small groups are so important is that they provide a context for the power of relationship to flourish. One of my mantras in group is, "No one heals alone." In other words, no one can give themselves what is needed to heal. As much as we need water and food, we also need the support of others in our lives. Our pain and struggles are based on wounds from relationships. Our group members come with very unique wounds, but they all boil down to a history of hurt and pain within relationships. Some of their ways of trying to meet their own needs have made matters worse, perhaps by learning to hurt others, making it difficult to experience mutually trusting relationships. Small groups give people a chance to develop close, trusting relationships with the leader and other members. These relationships help group members see how they engage in relationships and develop new habits and behaviors (e.g., accountability). For example, some people tend to pull inside themselves when they are in pain. They rarely get the support they need because the people who love them do not know what they need. Other people have trouble controlling their anger or sharing vulnerable emotions such as hurt, humiliation, or grief. People who love them might be scared to get close, even though they see the person suffering. Indeed, many people struggle to develop and maintain healthy relationships, and many people's problems are in some way related to their struggles in relationships. In a small group, members can work on developing intimate bonds with others, which can then be applied to other relationships outside the group.

The Role of Faith in Small Groups

I developed this model in my work within several Christian organizations, so part of my intent was to integrate small group work with a Christian worldview. Throughout the book, I link steps of The Healing Cycle with foundational themes from the Christian faith, such as grace, truth, and repentance. Even though I regularly draw on Christian language, the model and techniques can be used in secular settings or with other faith traditions. There is a history of mistrust between Christians and counseling and psychology. Thus, to help Christian group leaders who are evaluating the fit of this approach with their own faith, I include a section in each chapter that is explicitly focused on integrating the chapter's theme with principles from Christian scriptures. If you do not identify as Christian, I encourage you to read these sections as an example of how to evaluate the alignment of a therapeutic model with a faith tradition. After reading the first couple of chapters, if you find this section unhelpful, feel free to skip it in future chapters.

Application to Different Settings

The Healing Cycle is a versatile model for leading small groups that can be applied in a wide variety of settings. For example, you might be leading a church small group or Bible study. Your goal might be learning about a particular topic or book of the Bible, but you also might want to help group members apply this learning to their lives. Inevitably in a small group like this, your group members will be hurting and need support. You might want your small group to be a place where group members can bear one another's burdens and support each other (Galatians 6:2). The Healing Cycle can help you create a context where this can happen.

You might instead be a counselor who leads therapy groups, perhaps a general therapy group or a group focused on a particular psychological issue (e.g., depression, anxiety, or post-traumatic stress disorder). Like church groups often do, perhaps you have some educational material that you present, but you also really want the group to be a place for healing and growing. You want members to love and support each other toward lasting change and a greater sense of integrity. The Healing Cycle can help you become more effective as a group leader in this respect as well.

Leaders of a support group have members dealing with a particular problem, such as a struggling marriage, a divorce, or an addiction. The support group in some ways strikes a middle ground between a Bible study and therapy groups. Often there is a didactic component to support groups, but a major focus is giving people a place to share their painful struggles and have an opportunity to heal. In fact, I helped develop and implement The Healing Cycle in my work to train lay leaders to run support groups for people struggling with their marriages (Hook, Worthington, Hook, Miller, & Davis, 2011). Whatever group setting you find yourself in, my hope is that The Healing Cycle can provide you with a framework and relevant skills for helping your group members experience the healing and growth that can occur in a small group.

Structure of the Book

Each chapter of this book focuses on one step of The Healing Cycle. The chapters have a consistent structure to help you retain the material and easily locate and remind yourself of certain principles or techniques as you are running your groups. I give examples from a hypothetical group in order to illustrate what the skills and techniques look like in an actual group. In fact, the group members stay the same throughout the chapters, so you can follow them throughout the entire book. Although this group is fictional, everything I present is based on real experiences over the years.

Each chapter begins with a description of the step of The Healing Cycle, as well as some thoughts about why the topic is important—from a psychological and a Christian perspective. After that, I share an example of the group leader struggling with the step of The Healing Cycle. Leading small groups can be hard, and readers will likely connect with some of the examples presented. After explaining the example, I get into the meat of the chapter—the leader skills, practical skills that you can develop as a group leader to help bring about the healing and growth you long to see in your group members. Throughout each chapter I provide examples of the group working well, so that you can get a picture of what that looks like. Finally, I end each chapter with a series of exercises that you can complete individually and as a group. An ideal way to go through this book would be with other group leaders. You could then have the experience of being in a group as well as having support and accountability as you lead your own group.

Related to the suggestion about working through this book with other leaders, you may be leading a group by yourself or you may have a cofacilitator. If possible, I recommend leading with someone. I began leading groups by myself, but now I always try to lead with a cofacilitator. In my therapy groups, I have a cofacilitator who sits opposite me. That way we both have eyes on the whole group. When I lead marital groups at church with my wife, we sit together. Leading with someone is easier and less stressful than leading groups alone. My cofacilitator and I see different things, respond differently to group members, and bring different strengths to leading the group. It is also energizing to lead with someone. If you do have a cofacilitator, make sure you can work well together and are on the same page for how to lead the group. In the examples in this book, to make things easier for the reader, the group has just one leader.

As you work through the chapters in this book, you may feel like there is a lot of information to digest and process. Give yourself freedom to take in and apply this information at your own pace. You may only want to incorporate some of the suggestions now and leave others for a later time; that is okay. Some of the skills or activities may be beyond the scope of your particular small group or your skills as a group leader and facilitator. Pick and choose the skills and activities that you find useful in your group setting.

INTRODUCING THE GROUP

As I mentioned earlier, I share stories in each chapter from an example group so that you can begin to see how some leader skills look in practice. These examples can also provide a starting place for a beginning group leader on how to introduce topics or exercises to the group. As you read the examples, start by following what I say and then personalize the statements to your own voice.

The example group is from a church small group, similar to a Bible study or support group. In general, the group starts by introducing a particular topic or passage of scripture, and then the group discusses how to apply the passage to their individual lives and situations. In addition to learning, a major goal of the group is to provide a context for mutual support, healing, and growth to occur among group members. The group's goal isn't just to learn truth or content about God or the Bible, but to help members learn to apply it to their own lives. The group includes both men and women, with members at various ages and stages of life. The names and identifying information of the example group members have been changed, but the group members represent people and issues I have seen in my work leading small groups over the past thirty years.

The Group Members

Let me introduce you to the group members that you will meet throughout the book. Edward is a fifty-five-year-old man. As a very successful banking executive, he works very hard and is proud of his accomplishments. At his work he has a take-charge personality, and a large number of individuals report to him. At his job and at home, Edward can be aggressive and sometimes hostile. He is controlling and critical of his wife, which other group members see, but he is also very outgoing and charming. When we started the work in group, group members really liked Edward, but his relationships deteriorated as he started making critical and attacking comments after the first few meetings. Edward's interpersonal style is rooted in his relationship with his parents, especially his dad. Edward's father was very critical of Edward growing up, and Edward felt as if he was never able to please his dad. Edward's growing-up years were highly conflictual. His parents dealt with conflict through yelling and screaming—at each other and at Edward.

Jane and Edward are married. She is fifty-four years old. After they got married, Jane worked as a children's nurse for a few years until they had children, and then Jane stayed at home to raise her kids. She comes across as passive and a people-pleaser. She works hard to be sweet, kind, and supportive. She portrays herself as a martyr in her marriage. She is willing to sacrifice many of her own needs and wants for those of her husband and children. In group, she is very passive and rarely speaks unless directly asked a question. Although Jane and Edward both say they are happy in their marriage, I wonder whether Jane is able to speak up to Edward and get her needs met. Jane's parents were very traditional. Jane's father was the primary breadwinner, and Jane's mother was a homemaker. Jane felt a lot of pressure growing up to succeed in school and obey her parents, and she rarely rebelled or got in trouble.

Alice is a thirty-seven-year-old woman. She teaches junior high social studies. She comes across as put together and competent. When Alice shares, her comments are thoughtful and she doesn't seem to have a lot of overt difficulties or problems in her life. She tends to spiritualize things a lot, giving platitudes or other positive reframes when other group members describe their struggles. Alice is aware that she can be perfectionistic and controlling, which has caused problems in her marriage and her relationship with her kids. These behaviors have caused problems in group, because she struggles to empathize with others who are struggling or going through a difficult time. She tends to overspiritualize her own issues and has difficulty giving herself grace. Alice grew up in a family environment that tended to keep everything on the surface and avoid talking about deeper issues or problems. Also, she got involved in a church environment in high school that was very intense. Her religious and spiritual environment brought a lot of comfort and support to Alice growing up, but she also fell into the habit of using spiritual language to deflect or ignore some of her psychological and relational problems.

Ted, a forty-year-old man, is married to Alice. After graduating high school, Ted worked as a car salesman, and now he owns his own car dealership. His personality is loud and gregarious. He always has a joke or humorous story to tell. Ted likes to please and entertain everyone. Sometimes he dominates the conversation and doesn't seem to know when to back off. Initially he was great to have in group, because he was a very willing participant and always had something interesting to share about the topic. However, he can quickly become too much, and sometimes the other group members get frustrated with him. Ted grew up as the youngest of three siblings and often felt forgotten as a child. Ted's older brother was a star athlete in high school and his older sister had special needs, so both his siblings drew most of the attention. Also, Ted's dad wasn't around much growing up. He traveled a lot for work during the week and was often working even on the weekends.

Beth is a thirty-three-year-old woman. She is in graduate school, getting her master's degree in advertising. Beth is single, but was married for six years. She went through a divorce two years ago. She can be inconsistent and is habitually late for group. Beth is outgoing and talkative and tends to connect well with others, except for times when she becomes domineering and opinionated. She gets her feelings hurt easily. Thus, Beth vacillates between being outgoing and then withdrawing when experiencing conflict or hurt. Beth grew up in a large family with four siblings. Her parents were loving and did their best to care for their children, but the house was somewhat disorganized and chaotic. Beth's parents divorced when she was fifteen years old as a result of her father's extramarital affair, and their breakup was very upsetting to Beth.

James is a twenty-six-year-old single man who works as an engineer. He joined the group to feel more connected with other people at his church. Although he is bright and excels at work, he struggles in his relationships. He has few close friendships and has never had a serious dating relationship. James is quiet, introverted, and passive. He tends to stay in his head and intellectualizes all his emotions. Sometimes he seems to have difficulty connecting emotionally with the other group members, and he often comes across as distant. James's parents divorced when he was very young, and he never knew his biological father. James's mother struggled on and off with depression while James was growing up, and James never really felt connected to her or supported by her. James did well in school, but didn't participate in any after-school activities and struggled to connect with his classmates.

The Group Leader's Reactions

As you read through the examples, you may find that you are drawn to certain group members and that you have negative reactions toward other members. This is normal, also holding true for the groups that you lead. Based on your own cultural background, personality, history, and personal issues, you likely find it easier to connect with certain types of individuals.

Be aware of these tendencies, so that you can make an extra effort to connect with the group members who are more difficult for you, and be careful not to overidentify with other members. Also explore what about certain group members triggers or upsets you. Processing these reactions in supervision or with a peer can be helpful.

Sometimes the underlying issues of group members stay hidden in our groups. Members often don't want to expose the vulnerable and wounded parts of themselves right away. The examples I use may seem dramatic or intense, and you may think these kinds of issues are not present in the groups you lead. But once group members feel safe enough to share vulnerably, you will begin to see the pain and brokenness that lie beneath the personas that people present in public. Thus, I invite you to regularly remind yourself of the potential hurt and brokenness that people may conceal until they experience a culture of grace.

Moving Forward

Leading small groups is challenging work that sometimes feels like a struggle. At the same time, some of my most rewarding helping experiences have occurred in the small group context. I have seen group members save their failing marriages, break free from addictions, comfort one another in their struggles, and experience the grace of God. And now, thirty years after leading my first small group, it is the most exciting, challenging, and rewarding part of my week. I am excited to journey with you on your own process in becoming an effective small group leader.

Grace

GRACE IS THE FIRST step of The Healing Cycle. Grace is *unconditional acceptance*, and *acceptance* is a status of being included, embraced, valued, and part of a team. If you think back on your life to some of your most painful moments, they probably had something to do with not being accepted. Psychologist Abraham Maslow (1943) said that acceptance is a foundational need for humans, right after our physiological needs (e.g., food and water) and our personal safety. Lack of acceptance is one of the most painful experiences of the human condition. I remember one time as a kid when my teacher played a practical joke on me. I remember everyone laughing at me and how *not* accepted I felt, alone in my pain. Maybe you were picked last at gym class or rejected by a boyfriend or girlfriend. At our core, we all long for acceptance, and it is incredibly painful when we don't get it.

Grace is unconditional acceptance, which means granted without prerequisites. The person or situation may change, but acceptance does not, because it is based on the fact that a person has deep value and worth to the heart of God. This unconditional aspect of grace is deeply counterintuitive in our culture, because most relationships are conditional. From an early age, we learn that "you reap what you sow." If we do something good, we get rewarded and praised for it. If we do something bad, we get punished for it. At school, we learn the same thing. If we are good at basketball or physically attractive, we get praised. If we are awkward or overweight, we are mocked.

Because so much of life is based on conditional acceptance, we extend this template to core relationships with our family and even God. Even if our parents say they love us no matter what, we may not truly believe that if we did terrible things. Even if God says he loves us as a good father and nothing could separate us from his love (Romans 8:39), we might assume that this only applies if we stay within the requirements we have set up for our life—for example, reading our Bible enough, praying a lot, and avoiding too much sin.

The unconditional aspect of grace is the antidote to painful cycles of shame that can keep people from changing. Because it is so rare, the unconditional aspect of grace makes the grace culture in a group so powerful. It provides a basic need of the soul that group members have not been able to fulfill in any other aspect of their lives. In fact, in most areas of their lives, they probably experience the opposite of grace. The problem is that group leaders swim in the same water—a culture stripped of grace—so it is hard for us to make the shift to offering unconditional acceptance to group members without soaking in grace ourselves.

Psychology and Grace

Many psychological theories about how people grow and change incorporate ideas similar to grace. They may not use that exact term, but the idea of unconditional acceptance is central to their theories for how people make changes in their lives. The most famous example is Carl Rogers and his theory of person-centered therapy. Rogers was one of the founders of humanistic psychology, and he believed that each person was able to grow and reach their potential as long as they had the right environment (Rogers, 1957). One of the core components of this environment was being able to receive unconditional positive regard from others. Unconditional positive regard is very similar to the idea of grace—accepting, valuing, and loving a person for who they are. Positive regard is not taken away if the person does something wrong or makes a mistake—it is unconditional. Other psychological theories that have unconditional acceptance as a core component include mindfulness-based therapies (Baer, 2006) and acceptance and commitment therapy (ACT; Hayes, Luoma, Bond, Masuda, & Lillis, 2006).

CHRISTIANITY AND GRACE

A critique of the above theories is that they note the need for deep acceptance without articulating the basis for this acceptance. Within Christian spirituality, grace is based on the heart of God toward humans as expressed in the life of Jesus. When asked what he thought most clearly separated Christianity from other religions, C. S. Lewis' answer was grace (Yancey, 1997). Most religions teach that God gives acceptance in exchange for obedient and submissive behavior. Christianity teaches that people cannot become good until they experience transformational love from God. Our right standing before God is not based on our doing things, but on God's loving action. Before we had the wherewithal to even seek acceptance, God made a provision for sin through providing his own Son, so that we might become children of God, adopted as sons and daughters (Romans 8:14–16).

Healing and growth are all about grace. Scripture says that we are first "saved by God's grace" (Ephesians 2:8). God's grace picks us up out of our brokenness and enables us to "stand" (Romans 5:2). In the Psalms, King David wrote that God lifted him out of the slimy pit, out of the mud and mire, and set his feet on a rock, giving him a firm place to stand. And God gave him a new song to sing, a song of praise, a song that others would hear and cause them to turn to God (Psalm 40:2–3). Grace allows us to "grow" (2 Peter 3:18).

Grace ultimately comes from God. The apostle John wrote that "God is love" (1 John 4:16), and Jesus came to this earth "full of grace" (John 1:14). One beautiful illustration of Jesus giving grace involved a woman caught in adultery (John 8:1–11). According to the Torah, the punishment for adultery by a woman was death. The Pharisees brought the woman before Jesus and asked him what he thought. Even though the punishment for the offense was death, Jesus didn't just tell them about punishment. Instead, he said, "Let any one of you who is without sin be the first to throw a stone at her." Somehow the interaction caused every single accuser to realize that they were in no position to enforce justice. When all the Pharisees left, Jesus helped the woman to her feet and said, "Neither do I condemn you." The person who had every right to exclude instead offered acceptance. That's grace.

Jesus also told the woman to "go now and leave your life of sin." Grace did not leave her the same but called her to repentance, as I discuss in chapter 7. But grace came first. Jesus didn't begin by giving her a list of all the things she needed to do to get her life back on track. Attempting to change to earn acceptance is moralism, and moralism does not work. Shame runs too deep. Grace is acceptance that empowers change.

Our own experience with grace is connected with our ability to give grace to others. This point is illustrated beautifully in another story about Jesus and a "sinful" woman (probably a prostitute; Luke 7:36–50). The story begins with a Pharisee named Simon inviting Jesus over for dinner. They were reclining at the table when a sinful woman came into the house with a jar of perfume. She started to cry at the feet of Jesus, wiped her tears off his feet with her hair, and poured perfume on them.

The Pharisee reacted how I usually do when I see people do bad things—moral superiority and outrage. He said to himself, "If this man were a prophet, he would know who is touching him and what kind of woman she is—*that she is a sinner.*" The Pharisee didn't want to associate with a woman who was a sinner. Because he viewed sin as morally contagious, he had similar moral outrage toward Jesus.

But Jesus had a different perspective, and he told this parable: "Two people owed money to a certain moneylender. One owed him five hundred denarii [a denarius was the usual daily wage of a day laborer], and the other fifty. Neither of them had the money to pay him back, so he forgave the debts of both. Now which of them will love him more?"

In response, Simon correctly responded that the person who loved him more was the one with the bigger debt forgiven. Jesus then compares the sinful woman and Simon to the characters in the parable. He said, "Do you see this woman? I came into your house. You did not give me any water for my feet, but she wet my feet with her tears and wiped them with her hair. You did not give me a kiss, but this woman, from the time I entered, has not stopped kissing my feet. You did not put oil on my head, but she has poured perfume on my feet. Therefore, I tell you, her many sins have been forgiven—as her great love has shown. But whoever has been forgiven little loves little." Our ability to extend grace to others is proportional to our awareness of our own need for and ability to receive grace from God and others.

STRUGGLING WITH GRACE IN THE GROUP

"I have some thoughts on this topic," Ted quickly said as he raised his hand.

I nodded and forced a quick smile, inviting him to continue. As Ted began to share, however, I struggled to track with him and stay engaged. I looked around and noticed a few of the other group members had begun to check out also, which made me nervous and even angry. I worried that Ted's tendency to talk a lot might damage the cohesiveness of the group. I focused my attention back on Ted and tried to look for a place to move the conversation along to someone else. Ted finally paused to take a breath, and I quickly jumped in. "Thanks for sharing, Ted. Does anyone else want to comment on the passage?"

As the group ended for the night, as was customary, I said good-bye to all the group members and thanked them for their participation and contributions. When I got to Ted, I shook his hand and smiled. "See you next week, Ted. I really appreciate what you bring to the group." But the truth was that I was frustrated with him, and a part of me didn't even want him in the group. After all the group members left and I sat down to decompress, I tried to figure out why I struggled so much with Ted. It wasn't the first time I had gotten mad at him or wished he would just quit talking. I felt anxious because I knew I needed to allow other people to have a voice, but I also didn't want to hurt his feelings. Sometimes I would let him share and he would end up dominating the group. Other times, I would get up the courage to interrupt and redirect the conversation.

To make matters worse, each time Ted would share, I could feel my heart harden toward him a little more. I struggled to love or care for Ted in any sort of meaningful way. I didn't even want to ask him how he was doing. When I was able to get away from the situation and cool down a bit, I could understand that there was probably a reason Ted talked so much. He probably had pain and hurt, and while I knew that Ted needed grace and love from me and the group, I couldn't quite bring myself to give it to him. Instead, I usually would feel judgmental. Even though I managed to say the right things, on the inside I wanted to yell and tell Ted to stop. I knew this attitude probably came out in my nonverbal communication, but I couldn't seem to help myself. Although I really wanted to feel grace toward Ted, I just didn't, and I knew at some point he would see that.

This excerpt characterizes some of my early experiences leading small groups, and it took me awhile to learn what to do with my negative emotions toward group members. Group members can bring leaders face-to-face with the limits of our compassion and grace, for various reasons that I discuss later in this chapter. No matter how much you understand that your role as group leader is to cultivate a climate of grace, you still may feel judgment or anger. Part of you may secretly wish certain group members would just drop out. These feelings can cause a disconnect between your behavior in group and how you feel on the inside, which can be draining and limit your ability to lead. Even worse, you may start to feel stuck and not have any idea how to bring your heart and actions into greater alignment.

The purpose of this chapter is to help you develop a heart of grace toward your group members—even those members you find most difficult. Grace is foundational to the healing process, and it is essential for group members to experience grace—both from you as the leader and from other group members. However, many group leaders find it difficult to offer grace to all group members. Related to our difficulties offering grace to others, it is also sometimes difficult to offer and experience grace for ourselves.

Developing a Heart of Grace

As we experience and live in God's grace, we can begin to develop a heart of grace and offer grace to our group members. How much grace have you experienced? We can only give grace to the extent that we have experienced grace. The more we get grace and grow in our understanding of grace for ourselves, the more we can give grace to others.

The Healing Cycle begins with the need for and experience of grace. Think back to a time when you were struggling or experiencing brokenness and pain. When you reflect and think about what you really needed, deep down, it is likely that you needed someone to give you grace. You may not have been able to give yourself grace in your time of brokenness, because you were experiencing too much pain. You needed someone outside of yourself to accept and love you in your time of need.

Unfortunately, you may have experienced the opposite of grace. Maybe in your time of need, you didn't have anyone by your side and you were alone in your pain. If someone did show up, you may have experienced advice, criticism, or judgment instead of grace. Judgment and criticism communicate that you are not accepted as you are. Advice puts conditions on your acceptance, by saying that acceptance might be given, but only if you do certain things. When you experienced judgment, criticism, or advice, what did you do? You may have shut down, become isolated, and stayed stuck in your pain. Perhaps you lashed out and attacked someone close to you, or maybe you tried to avoid your pain by acting out with an addiction or something else to distract you.

The only real way out of pain is to share your brokenness with someone who can give you grace. If you share your pain and brokenness and receive judgment back, you are in an even worse position. What you need is to experience grace, which is true of your group members as well. They come experiencing various kinds of brokenness and pain—whether it is anxiety, depression, relationship problems with their spouse or kids, or feeling distant from God. Your group members cannot give grace to themselves. To start the healing process, they need to sit for a while in a culture of grace that values them in spite of their limitations.

As a group leader, you have to get grace, because it is so foundational to healing and growth. You get grace not through reading books or talking about it, but through abiding in cultures of grace—enjoying the freedom of being fully known and deeply loved. You begin to apply this experience of grace to every moment of disconnection, defensiveness, and isolation that you experience. If you don't experience grace for yourself, you'll find it difficult to offer grace to your group members. However, when you know grace for yourself, you can pass that grace on to others. The apostle Paul wrote that God, "the Father of compassion and the God of all comfort, . . . comforts us in all our troubles, so that we can comfort those in any trouble with the comfort we ourselves have received from God" (2 Corinthians 1:3–4). If you are relying on grace from God and others in your time of brokenness and pain, you can in turn give grace to others. From the grace you have received, you can extend grace to the participants in your group.

You do not have to have the exact same experience of brokenness as your group members in order to connect with them and give them grace, but you do need to get grace for yourself in your own areas of brokenness. For example, I do not need to be a sex addict in order to offer grace and work with the sex addicts in my therapy group (Hook, Hook, & Hines, 2008). But it is helpful for me to understand that sex is a struggle for everyone and that, like everyone, I have brokenness when it comes to sex. Everyone has their areas of brokenness, addictions, or "thorns in the flesh" that just won't go away (2 Corinthians 12:7). As you experience grace from God for your own brokenness, you will have comfort for those in any trouble.

HEART SKILLS

As a leader you need to develop a heart of grace, and in this section, I present three heart skills to help you. The heart skills involve getting in touch with and being able to share your experiences of brokenness, grace, and healing, but before I introduce the heart skills, I want to say a few words about appropriate self-disclosure as the group leader.

In what follows, you will complete some exercises to better understand your own stories of brokenness, grace, and healing. Part of this work is to help you develop a more grace-filled stance toward your group members, but you can also use your stories to model these concepts for your group members. In general, I believe leader self-disclosure can be a helpful tool as long as it is brief and purposeful. Self-disclosure should be short and used to model the concepts discussed in group, rather than to do your own work. (You need your own group for that.) Self-disclosure may be more or less appropriate in various settings (e.g., clinical settings vs. church settings). I do invite you, however, to think about increasing your use of self-disclosure to the extent you are comfortable with it.

Brokenness

The first heart skill involves getting in touch with and being able to share your story of brokenness. Leaders often believe that they need to set an example for their group members in regard to purity or good behavior. Group leaders might think, *If the people in my group really knew about my brokenness and struggle, they wouldn't respect me as a leader*, but that perspective doesn't match reality. As leaders, we struggle with pain and brokenness, just like our members. When we hide our story of brokenness, we set an unrealistic standard that everyone in the group should be perfect. Group members then follow our lead, only sharing the good parts of themselves and hiding their own areas of brokenness and pain. Very little real healing and growth happen in this type of group.

Instead of trying to set an unrealistic example of purity or good behavior, be a leader who sets an example in honesty and vulnerability. To do that, you need to be in touch with your own story of brokenness and pain—the ways you have been wounded or sinned against. Also, you need to acknowledge how you have coped with your brokenness and pain in unhealthy and sinful ways. Finally, you need to be in touch with the ways you have wounded or sinned against others.

We Have Been Wounded and Sinned Against

We all have been wounded or sinned against. We live in a fallen world, even if we don't always like to acknowledge it. In *The Sacred Romance*, authors Brent Curtis and John Eldridge (1997) write about being wounded by "arrows" in our lives. We all have painful experiences that are lodged deep into our memories and have shaped who we are. Jesus said, "In this world you will have trouble" (John 16:33). In the Christian story, pain and brokenness in the world go back to the fall. Because of sin, the "ground" became "cursed" (Genesis 3:17). Throughout the history of the world and continuing today, every single person experiences emotional pain and suffering. Families fall apart. Houses are destroyed by tornadoes. Loved ones are diagnosed with cancer. Children get sick and die. Every life has a portion of pain, suffering, and brokenness. One of my greatest wounding experiences was when my son had health problems when he was born. One of the most exciting and anticipated days of my life turned into one of the scariest experiences I have faced. A few years ago, I was diagnosed with prostate cancer and had to go through a difficult treatment process. What is your experience?

_____

_____

_____

Also, no matter how great a family you grew up in, you had imperfect parents and an imperfect family, and you likely did not get all the love and affirmation you needed. I grew up in a Christian family. My parents were missionaries overseas, but they weren't perfect. I experienced wounds in my childhood. My dad traveled a lot and wasn't home much. Because he wasn't involved in my life during my early years, I experienced abandonment instead of love. As was typical for missionary families back then, I was sent to boarding school in first grade and experienced more abandonment. When I was beginning high school, my parents left me in the United States, where I lived with my brother in a mission home for the rest of my high school years.

I only saw my parents and other siblings after graduating from high school. During my growing-up years, I moved around and lost friends, experiencing still more abandonment. These were some of my wounds.

For a long time, I struggled to own the wounds I received. My parents were doing the Lord's work, so how could I think or say anything negative about that? So I hid my brokenness and wounds, but hiding and denying them didn't work. In order to heal, I needed to own the wounds that I received. You also need to be able to own the wounds you have received from others. You have been sinned against. The sin you received may or may not have been intentional. Most of the abandonment in my life was unintentional, yet it was my experience, which I need to acknowledge.

Think back on your experiences, growing up in your family of origin. Spend some time reflecting on your story of brokenness. How were you wounded? How were you sinned against? Pick one wound that you might explore.

_____

_____

_____

Now think about how people responded to you growing up. When you experienced pain and reached out to the people closest to you, did you receive grace? Were you comforted? Or did you receive judgment, criticism, or advice? Were you told, "Boys don't cry," or "Pull yourself together"? To the degree that you received grace and comfort growing up, you probably understand grace today. However, the opposite is also true.

Boarding school was a lonely place for me. When bad stuff happened, there was no one I believed I could go to for comfort. I was alone in my pain. When you were little and in need of grace and comfort, what happened? Who comforted you? How was that experience? When there wasn't someone there to comfort you, what was that experience like?

_____

_____

_____

We Have Coped with Our Pain in Unhealthy Ways

When we are sinned against, we tend to react. Without comfort or help from others, we need some way to protect ourselves. Generally, people use one of two responses: violence or silence (Patterson, Grenny, McMillan, & Switzler, 2002). These coping mechanisms can numb us from pain, but they do not ultimately meet our need for love and comfort. They are ways we escape from our pain, but they are not healthy. As a result, we stay broken by our sins against ourselves.

In the story of Adam and Eve, after Adam and Eve sinned, they hid from God among the trees and went to silence (Genesis 3). Instead of having an open relationship with God, God had to come looking for them. Adam and Eve also hid from each other by creating clothes made from fig leaves. Instead of being naked and unashamed, there was now separation between them. Instead of open intimacy, there was a barrier. We, too, have this tendency to hide when we are sinned against, and when we sin against others. We hide and withdraw from God, and we put on masks to hide so that others won't know our pain and brokenness.

God intervened in order to cut past the defenses and meet the need for grace. When God found Adam and Eve hiding and confronted them, they blamed and attacked. Adam blamed Eve, and he also blamed God. He said, "It's the fault of the woman you put here with me" (Genesis 3:12 NIrV). And when Eve was confronted, she blamed the serpent. We also tend to blame others and God for our sin. If our strategies of hiding and blaming don't work, we might numb the pain and escape by going to our addictions.

When I experienced pain and brokenness growing up, my primary response was to isolate. Also, because I felt abandoned growing up, I tended to think that I was on my own in life. I believed I couldn't rely on anyone except myself. I coped by becoming independent, and still today I withdraw, even from those who are closest to me.

One of my most painful experiences was when my son was born. My wife and I had been looking forward to his birth with so much anticipation, and when it finally happened, I was overwhelmed with wonder and gratitude. It was a very special moment. He was born in the morning, and I had been up all night alongside my wife as she went through a very difficult labor. I was exhausted, so I went home to get some sleep after making some excited phone calls to our families.

When I came back to the hospital, I discovered that my son Josh seemed to be in serious trouble. The hospital staff was working on him in order to keep him alive and breathing. In an instant, this most happy episode in my life became the most scary and out of control. I had to sign papers releasing him and the doctors to try and figure out the problem, and he was sent off to another hospital where he could receive the appropriate care. I will never forget how scared I felt. Here I was experiencing brokenness because of a fallen world.

My first response was to isolate. I felt depressed. I was angry at myself, thinking that somehow it might have been my fault that this happened. And then I looked outside myself, to blame someone else for the pain in my life. I went to violence. I got mad at God for making this happen. I raged. We had been trying so long to have a child. How could a loving God let us feel all this joy and hope, only to crush us if our child didn't make it?

Take some time and think about how you react when you experience pain and brokenness. What has been your way of coping? Do you tend to hide and withdraw? Or do you attack and blame? Or maybe you have an addiction that you escape to?

_____

_____

_____

We Have Wounded and Sinned against Others
In addition to receiving wounds and being sinned against, you have also wounded and sinned against others. No matter how hard you have tried to be good, sometimes you have been the one doing the wounding. For the entire history of humankind,

we have all sinned against others. The Christian story of the creation of the world paints a picture of the universal experience of sinning against others. Adam and Eve were in a perfect loving relationship with each other and with God, but they chose to live life their own way instead of living life God's way. And when they went their own way, they sinned. They separated themselves from God. It didn't take long before sin involved violence and murder against our fellow man (Genesis 4).

By isolating and withdrawing in order to cope with my son's birth difficulties, I pulled away from my wife, Cheryl, as well. My withdrawal was hurtful to her. I sinned against her. It wasn't intentional, but much of the sin that comes out of our brokenness is not intentional. It is us trying to protect ourselves, but in doing so, we pass on our brokenness.

Think about the ways you have coped with your brokenness, but in coping, you have wounded and sinned against others. How have you hurt others who are close to you? How have you acted in ways that are selfish and unloving toward your family, friends, and coworkers? How have your silence, violence, or addictions hurt others?

_____

_____

_____

By writing out and trying to understand your story of brokenness, you have gifts to offer the participants in your group. Sharing your brokenness shows your group members that you are one of them. You are a leader, but you are not above being wounded. You can relate. And your story continues with your experience of grace.

Grace

The second heart skill involves getting in touch with and being able to share your story of grace, which is often closely linked to your story of brokenness. In your most intense moments of brokenness and pain, you probably felt as if you didn't deserve love or acceptance. You may have felt as if you were beyond hope. At these moments, grace is so powerful. In your worst and most painful times, you may not have deserved it, but you received acceptance and love anyway.

Your story of grace likely involves experiencing grace from God and others. Perhaps there was a time in your brokenness and pain when you reached out to God and felt comforted. Maybe there was a story in the Bible or a particular passage of scripture that you strongly connected with, and felt as if God was speaking directly to you. There may have been a particular time during prayer or worship when you felt particularly comforted by God, even in the midst of your brokenness. During the time of my son's birth problems, unfortunately I wasn't very aware of God's grace. I know in hindsight about his grace, but at the time I was too caught up in my own pain.

Think back to your story of brokenness. Where was God during this time? Can you think of a time where you felt God give you grace in your brokenness?

Sometimes it is difficult to experience grace from God. Maybe you have struggled with this in your own life. You might read verses in the Bible saying that God is gracious, God is merciful, and God loves you. But for some reason, you don't *feel* grace from God. There is a disconnection between what you know intellectually about God and what you personally experience.

Part of the reason for this difficulty is that our ways of thinking and behaving in relationships carry over into our relationship with God (McDonald, Beck, Allison, & Norsworthy, 2005). So, for example, if our earthly fathers abandoned us when we were little, we might worry that God will abandon us also. If our mothers criticized and judged us harshly when we messed up or did something wrong, we probably expect God to be the same way. I know that, for me, my relationship with my dad hurt my relationship with God. For years, I had a deistic view of God. I believed that God created the world and kept it going, but then kind of checked out. Although I grew up having prayed the prayer and believed I was a Christian, I had little belief in a God who really cared about me and wanted a relationship with me. As a result, I didn't experience much of God's grace. It has been an ongoing journey to see God differently and experience God as intimately involved in my life and offering me grace. Unfortunately, many of us haven't experienced much grace in our families of origin or even in our churches. Because of that, we may not experience much grace in our relationship with God, even if we know in our head that God is gracious and loving.

That's why relationships where we experience grace are so important. Receiving grace from others can help correct our experience of what God is like. Receiving grace from others also challenges our other life experiences of judgment, criticism, and advice. God usually helps us know grace through relationships. For example, when I was struggling after my son was taken to a different hospital for more intensive treatment, my brother showed up. In my pain, brokenness, and isolation, he was there with me. He listened to me and put his arm around my shoulder. Through his words and actions, he communicated grace to me. I was accepted, in my messiness, just how I was. My growth in grace took a big step with my brother giving me grace. I began to slowly get involved with other men and experienced their grace, too. It opened a pathway where I now get and am able to receive God's grace, like I started to develop a muscle for grace that wasn't previously there.

Think about your own life, especially your areas of brokenness. How has God used other people to offer you grace in your time of need? How have you experienced grace in your relationships with others?

_____

_____

_____

Healing

The third heart skill involves being in touch with and being able to share your ongoing story of healing. You have experienced brokenness and grace in your relationships, and there you also have a story of ongoing healing and growth.

In order to lead your group effectively, you need to have experienced some healing from your brokenness and pain, which does not mean being perfect. Healing is an ongoing process rather than a onetime event. You will always have scars and you will be vulnerable in your area of brokenness. But to comfort others, you need to have experienced some healing. Otherwise, others' needs will trigger your own areas of brokenness and leave you emotionally unavailable to bring grace and comfort.

The apostle Paul talks about this balance in his letter to the church in Galatia. In chapter 6, he wrote, "Brothers and sisters, if someone is caught in a sin, you who live by the Spirit should restore that person gently. But watch yourselves, or you also may be tempted" (Galatians 6:1). Paul encourages leaders to engage while also remaining vigilant to their own areas of weakness. As a leader, you will always need to do your own work. Your healing around your brokenness is never completely finished.

Paul understood this ongoing process of healing in his own life. He called it a "thorn in the flesh" (2 Corinthians 12:7). Interestingly Paul never tells the reader what specifically the thorn was. In a way, this not knowing is a gift for us, because we can think about our own thorn and connect with Paul's experience. When you think of your area of brokenness, how many times have you prayed for healing, and despite your prayer, your brokenness continues to surface in your life? Paul prayed three times for his thorn to be removed. This number could mean that Paul literally prayed three times, but another interpretation is that Paul prayed indefinitely for his thorn to be removed—yet it was not.

We might pray consistently for our brokenness to be removed from our life, but for many of us, our brokenness remains a part of who we are until we die. When Paul asked for his thorn to be removed, God's response was, "My grace is sufficient for you, for my power is made perfect in weakness" (2 Corinthians 12:9). God saw purpose in Paul's brokenness. Paul's ongoing story of brokenness and healing allowed him to more fully understand and experience God's grace. Because of Paul's thorn, he was also able to be a person who brought grace and comfort to others. Like Paul, our thorn—our ongoing story of healing—is a gift. It allows us to more fully experience and depend upon God's grace and mercy, which enables us to be ministers of God's grace to others, especially people in the groups.

In regard to my area of brokenness, I still have the tendency to feel abandoned and to isolate. Ask my wife. When something bad happens, isolation is my initial response, which can be hurtful to her. My isolation is also hurtful to me. But this thorn does draw me to God. It puts me in a place where I need to rely on God's grace, and I need to understand that God's grace is sufficient for me. My ongoing story of healing also gives me the opportunity to grow in grace and to do life differently. It puts me in a place where I have an opportunity to reach out to others instead of to isolate. It offers me a growing and healing experience if I am willing to take advantage of it. My story of healing is what I have to offer the participants in my groups.

Think about your ongoing story of healing. What is the thorn in your flesh? Might God be using that thorn to help you under-stand and experience grace? What about your ongoing story of healing can you offer your group members?

HEART SKILLS IN ACTION

How do these heart skills get played out in your group? By own-ing your brokenness, understanding your own experience of grace, and engaging in your own ongoing process of healing, as a leader you can extend grace to your participants. You know and understand that everyone is wounded. The brokenness of your group members does not surprise or shock you. With some group members, their brokenness and need for grace is obvious. Others may hide their brokenness, but their masks do not fool you. You know that they are broken because you understand your own brokenness. Having experienced grace yourself from both God and others, you in turn have grace for their areas of brokenness. You regularly show grace by accepting them where they are, without putting conditions on your acceptance. You are able to show interest in your participants' stories, whatever their pain. You listen. You are patient and able to empathize. You are able to extend grace because you have experienced grace.

Pay attention to instances in which you struggle to give grace to your group members. If we are open, these individuals can be a gift for us, spurring on more healing and growth in our own lives. In fact, the individuals to whom we struggle to give grace often are connected to our own areas of brokenness in some way. These group members might be similar to people who have hurt us in the past, or some part of these group members is similar to something we struggle with ourselves. Either way, these difficult group members can be an invitation to further explore our own stories of brokenness, grace, and healing.

GRACE IN THE GROUP

From the very first group meeting, I knew I would have a difficult time with Ted. Right from the start, he was very talkative and outgoing, dominating the conversation and the meeting. My story was that he was just trying to get attention. I wanted him to quit showing off. My natural response and reaction toward Ted was not grace but anger. I would finish the group meetings and be almost seething on the inside because I was so mad. I felt like he was ruining the group experience for the other group members (and myself).

Once I realized I was having a strong reaction to Ted, I asked myself why. *Why am I having this kind of reaction? Why don't I want to extend grace to Ted? What is it about Ted that is such a trigger for me?* Reflecting on this question opened the door for some work in my own life. I realized that Ted reminded me of my father. My father was a missionary and a preacher, and he talked a lot. If I ever asked my dad a question, I usually got a sermon. I didn't feel like he really listened to me; instead, I felt like he only cared about getting his point across. As this started to become a pattern in our interactions, I began to turn him off like a light switch whenever he talked. In fact, after a while, I stopped asking him questions so that I wouldn't get a sermon.

I was able to share my struggle with a colleague and do some work in dealing with my own anger toward my dad, as well as my sadness and loss about him not being there to support me when I needed him. I was able to own my own brokenness in my lack of connection to my dad. I also became aware of my own tendency to talk too much and preach, much like he did. I was able to give grace to myself and receive grace from God. I also received grace from my colleague, who understood where I was coming from and loved and accepted me right where I was. I was able to do some work on forgiving my dad and realizing the story of his life and his own brokenness. Even though he was already dead, I could forgive him.

As I worked toward my own healing, I found increased space in my heart to give grace to people like Ted, even when they did things that triggered me. During the group meetings, I became more patient with and able to listen to him. It still annoyed me some that he talked a lot, but I also was able to listen beneath his talking and hear his pain. I could see how his many words only partially masked what was really happening in his heart. I found myself becoming less judgmental of Ted and able to accept him where he was at, as he entered into the group process to do his own work. I was able to accept the fact that he was broken, needed grace, and was in process in his healing (just like me).

GRACE EXERCISES: INDIVIDUAL

What is your story of brokenness? What is your story of grace? What is your ongoing story of healing? One way to help develop a heart of grace is to write out your story. Your own personal story of brokenness, grace, and healing is what you have to offer the people in your group who are broken. Again, the more that you get grace, the more you will be able to offer grace to your group members.

In this next exercise, think back on your life to one event in which you experienced a great deal of brokenness—a time that you still feel has emotional power over you or represents an ongoing struggle for you, like Paul's thorn in the flesh. Take a clean sheet of paper, and spend some time journaling, using the following topics as a guide.

- Title of event: Give the event a name (e.g., physical abuse).
- What happened? Briefly summarize the circumstances surrounding the event.
- Feelings: Write the feelings you have associated with what happened (e.g., sad, angry, scared, happy, excited, tender).
- Message(s): What message did you tell yourself at the time? What messages do you continue to tell yourself even today (e.g., I am _____)?
- Coping: How did you cope with what happened? Did you go to silence or violence?
- Addictions: What addictions or other methods of self-soothing did you turn to?
- Impact: How does this event continue to impact you even today (e.g., your "fate" in life)?

- Grace: How have you experienced grace surrounding this event?
- Healing: What does your ongoing process of healing look like?

This is your story of brokenness, grace, and healing. This is a historical story, meaning it happened in the past, but it is also an ongoing story, meaning it continues to affect you even today. Every week you have your story to offer the people in your group. As you do your own work of healing and growth, you have the opportunity to offer your work as a gift to your group members. You can lead from a place of brokenness, grace, and healing.

The heart skills discussed in this chapter are brokenness, grace, and healing. On another piece of paper, assess your heart skills. Which heart skills are a strength for you? Which heart skills do you need to work on and develop? When you lead, what kinds of people do you find difficult? Why do you have trouble extending grace to these kinds of people? How are these people gifts for you in your ongoing process of becoming a person who embodies grace? Are you aware of your ongoing need for work in these areas? How are you doing your work? Where are you getting support for your own work so that you can keep growing in these areas in order to be fully available to lead your group? Write down your growth edge for grace.

_____

_____

_____

GRACE EXERCISE: GROUP

If you are working through this book as part of training with other readers, complete this group exercise focused on your stories of brokenness, grace, and healing. This exercise can push you to give grace to yourself in a new way and also give you the opportunity to practice giving grace to others. After writing down your experiences of brokenness, grace, and healing, I invite you to share your stories with each other. Right now, if you are in a small group, take some time to share your story of brokenness: what happened, your feelings, and the stories and messages that you made up about yourself. Share how you coped with what happened. Finally, share how this story still impacts you today. As each person shares, the rest of the group should just listen. Don't give any comments, feedback, or advice. Just listen. At the end, thank the person for sharing. Go around the group until each person has shared a story of their brokenness.

After each person has shared, go around the circle again and share one way you have experienced grace from God about this event, as well as one way you have experienced grace from another person about this event. Perhaps you have only experienced a little bit of grace, and that's okay. Again, as one person shares a story of grace, the rest of the group should just listen, without giving any comments, feedback, or advice. Again, thank the person for sharing their story. Do the same thing with your own ongoing story of healing.

After each person in the group has shared a story of brokenness, grace, and healing, take some time to reflect. What was it like to share those stories? If your group is like most groups, it may have been difficult and felt too vulnerable. What did it feel like to share your story and have people listen without judging, criticizing, or giving advice? What was it like to just listen to the other people's stories? Was it hard for you to refrain from judging, criticizing, or giving advice? After sharing, did you feel more or less connected with the other people in your group? After sharing, did you trust the people in your group more or less?

_____

_____

_____

Safety

SAFETY IS THE SECOND step of The Healing Cycle. Safety involves feeling secure and protected from danger, as well as an openness and freedom to explore and try new things. Doing any personal work is difficult when we feel unsafe or are experiencing a large amount of fear and anxiety. When this fear and anxiety become overwhelming, we are more likely to close up to protect ourselves. Group members who feel unsafe are not usually able to share vulnerably or engage with the other group members. On the other hand, a group in which safety is promoted and maintained is one where healing and growth can flourish.

One important distinction when leading small groups is the difference between feeling discomfort and feeling unsafe. Participating in a group experience and sharing vulnerably naturally leads to some fear, anxiety, and discomfort. Some discomfort is a good thing, letting people know that something important is happening in the group. Group members, as a result, are encouraged to lean into, rather than avoid, their feelings of discomfort, because that is how growth happens. Too much discomfort occurs when people perceive that they are unable to effectively tolerate the distress. Accordingly, they feel unsafe, which can cause debilitating fear and anxiety and undermine growth.

Striking the right balance between discomfort and safety is similar to the practice of yoga. In yoga, you engage in a progression of stretches and holding positions. These positions are uncomfortable in the short term, but over time, increasing your tolerance for discomfort makes your muscles stronger and more resilient. Of course, one key in yoga is not pushing yourself too hard, which could lead to injury. Pulling a muscle would take you out of your exercise routine for a while. In our groups, we want that yogalike discomfort. We want people to lean into discomfort, but in a safe way.

Psychology and Safety

Many psychologists have discussed the importance of safety in leading happy, full lives. Psychologist Abraham Maslow (1943) said that safety was one of our foundational needs as human beings—second only to the physiological needs of food, water, and sleep. Safety has to be in place for work, play, and love to occur.

The professions of counseling and psychotherapy put several rules into place to increase safety. For example, all counseling involves confidentiality. In the first session, clients learn that, with few exceptions, what they share in counseling will not be shared with others. These rules are supported by laws and codes of ethics (American Psychological Association, 2002). The client doesn't have to worry that things shared in counseling will somehow be spilled to one's friends or the general public. Also, certain boundaries are set in place around the counseling session. For example, most of the time, people attend counseling on the same day and time each week. Each session lasts a predetermined amount of time. All of these rules help establish a greater sense of safety so that clients can share vulnerably without fear of negative consequences.

In group therapy, counselors usually ask group members to agree to rules designed to promote a sense of safety (Bernard et al., 2008). Sometimes they even have group members sign a contract. Having a set of agreed-upon ground rules is one of the most important ways to create safety in your group. Rules help clients know how to expect to be treated. Counselors also clarify what happens if someone breaks the rules. This structure creates a sense of safety in the group. In the section on boundaries, I go over some of the main rules I suggest when leading your own small groups.

Christianity and Safety

Christianity has a lot to say about safety, fear, and anxiety. The Bible encourages us to feel safe and secure in our relationship with God. In his letter to the Philippians, Paul encourages us to "not be anxious about anything, but in every situation, by prayer and petition, with thanksgiving, present your requests to God" (Philippians 4:6). When people were struggling with worry, Jesus encouraged them by telling them to consider the birds in the air and the flowers in the field (Matthew 6). If God takes care of the needs of birds and adorns the flowers with beauty, then we can count on God to care for our needs.

Rules and guidelines have always been a part of Christian spirituality. In the Old Testament, the Israelites were called to follow the Ten Commandments, as well as a plethora of other rules that protected and governed their relationship with God and each other. In the New Testament, Jesus explained that he came not to abolish the law but to fulfill it (Matthew 5:17). Jesus said that the entire point of the law is to promote love of God and neighbor (Matthew 22:37–39). Indeed, he said, "All the Law and the Prophets hang on these two commandments" (Matthew 22:40). Rules and boundaries serve a similar function in your group. They provide a context for your clients to learn to love God and each other more deeply. Rules are not there to promote perfectionistic striving; they are there to create safety, so that group members can pursue healing and growth.

Creating a context of grace and safety helps reduce fear and anxiety so that group members can share vulnerably. The Bible says, "There is no fear in love. But perfect love drives out fear" (1 John 4:18). Safe, grace-filled relationships help drive out fear. To be able to share vulnerably in the group, your group members need safe, loving, grace-filled relationships.

STRUGGLING WITH SAFETY IN THE GROUP

Threats to safety can happen quickly in a group. During one group meeting, we were discussing the parable of the Prodigal Son, and Alice was sharing some of her thoughts. Alice often relates insightful comments but she tends to spiritualize, and her sharing comes across as judgmental. Instead of sharing vulnerably and receiving support for her comments, her spiritualized statements tend to create distance and can be off-putting. Alice displayed this relational pattern in group this week. As it turned out, she had just finished listening to a book on tape by pastor Tim Keller (2008) on the story of the Prodigal Son, and she was excitedly relating what she had learned from the book. However, she wasn't sharing much about her own life and how she could apply the story to her own work. Instead, she shared about her intellectual understanding of the story as well as how it applied to other people in her life.

As I was listening to Alice and watching the group, I began to look for a way to redirect her sharing toward herself and her own work. I was struggling, however, to make a smooth transition, because Alice seemed to be pretty defensive about sharing anything related to her own pain and struggle. One time I tried to intervene, asking which of the two brothers in the story she identified with more. Even here she struggled to bring the focus to herself, talking about the story more broadly as a metaphor for God's love and humanity's tendency to go off track.

Other people were also getting irritated with Alice's tendency to overspiritualize. Edward was one member of the group who never had trouble speaking his mind. Normally this was a good thing, but sometimes he could blow up and react in anger. After Alice had gone on for a few minutes without sharing anything about herself or what she was working on, Edward had enough and jumped in. "Alice, can't you see that you're doing it again? You're going on and on, but you aren't really doing any real work. Stop giving us a sermon and share something about yourself."

The group fell silent. Alice's face got red. She pursed her lips and then reclined back in her chair. There was an awkward silence, and Edward, feeling embarrassed about his outburst, muttered a quick apology. "I'm sorry, Alice, I didn't mean that. I just wanted us to get back to sharing about ourselves. I can read the book myself if I want to."

The awkward silence continued, and no one said anything. Most group members looked down at the floor, trying not to make eye contact with each other. Other group members looked at me, wondering what I would do as the leader. I thought I should say something, but I wasn't sure what to say. I agreed with some of what Edward said, although he probably could have said it in a kinder way. Feeling anxious and still not knowing what to say, I asked the next discussion question to change the subject. The group continued, but I knew people were thinking about what happened.

Unfortunately, this situation is quite common in small groups. Group members are human beings, just like leaders, with their own problems, issues, and triggers. Group members bring their full selves to their group interactions. Most of the time this is a good thing, but sometimes group members do things that make other group members feel unsafe. They might interrupt or criticize another group member, like Edward did. They might focus on other people and not do their own work, like Alice. They might break confidentiality and share another member's private information outside of the group. They might arrive late or even miss several group sessions. All these actions can damage the sense of safety in your group.

Creating and Maintaining Safety

As your group members experience grace, they will begin to feel safe in their relationship with you and others in your small group. To heal and grow, group members must feel safe. Think of your role like a gardener. A lot goes into helping plants grow and flourish. In the same way, people need some key ingredients in order to grow. For example, people have personal resources and support systems that they bring to the group, and then there are the discussions and interpersonal interactions that happen in the group. The Holy Spirit is active in the group and in the lives of the group members. However, certain weeds can also slow the growth of the group and perhaps even choke out its life. In this chapter, I discuss skills that you can develop to establish and maintain boundaries that optimize the potential for group members to feel safe and grow.

Sometimes I wish I lived in a condominium, because then someone else would keep my yard for me. But I live in a house, and my yard requires consistent upkeep in order to stay healthy. Grass needs to be cut. Gardens need weeding. Storms cause tree limbs to fall that must be picked up. The maintenance never ends. But we were created to create and tend to God's creation (Genesis 1:26–30), so there is something deeply rewarding about creating and maintaining a well-ordered space. Also, when the day is over, it feels good to rest and enjoy the beauty of nature and my work. The group leader's role is similar. If left alone, groups do not automatically become places of safety and order, but with careful and loving attention, you can learn to create and maintain certain group structures or habits that promote thriving in its members.

Safety is important throughout the group process, but especially in the beginning stages, when norms are most malleable. For individuals, especially in groups, it is hard to change bad habits once they are established. This phase is often called the "forming stage" of a group (Tuckman, 1965). People entering the group are wondering how the group is run and what is expected of them. No matter how much experience they have in prior groups, this group is new, and new experiences trigger anxiety. Participants do not vulnerably share their stories of brokenness with each other without feeling safe.

Before we get into what safety looks like in group, go back to the experience of brokenness you wrote about in the previous chapter. What was the time and place where you experienced the most pain and brokenness? Once you have reflected on that experience for a bit, imagine sharing your story of brokenness in a small group of people you didn't know well. What do you feel when you think of sharing your pain?

_____

_____

_____

If you are anything like me, you probably feel scared or afraid. What is your fear about as you think of bringing your brokenness into relationship with others?

For many of us, the greatest fear is being judged or criticized. Men in my sex addiction group are afraid that if they share everything, others will think they are sick, pathetic, disgusting, or weak. If you are experiencing brokenness in your relationships and your marriage is falling apart, you might be afraid of judgments that you are bad and of experiencing rejection. Group members in my Bible study are scared to go deeper for a variety of reasons. Staying superficial is much easier but does not bring about healing and growth. You were broken in relationship and you will be healed in relationship, if you bring your story of brokenness into relationship. This only occurs when you feel safe.

Fear gets in the way of me sharing more deeply. When I think back to my experience of brokenness, I believed that I should be able to handle my pain by myself. I thought that bringing my pain into relationship with others would be a sign of weakness. Because I judged myself that way, it is natural that I anticipated similar judgment from others, too, so I hesitated to share my pain. When I was struggling around the circumstances of my son's birth, I hesitated to tell my brother how scared and out of control I felt when he visited me in the hospital. He might have judged that I was weak.

Safety in a small group doesn't just happen. As the leader, you must develop, cultivate, and maintain safety. After developing a heart of grace, creating and maintaining safety is the group leader's most important task. Here I discuss two sets of skills for creating and maintaining safety. The first set of skills involves setting boundaries or rules about the group and its process. When you lead a small group, you are creating a container for your members to hold whatever is brought to the group. The container must be strong and safe enough to deal with the pain that its members share. Boundaries are like a wall or barrier that can keep out the bad and keep in the good (Cloud & Townsend, 1992); they create the structure that helps your group feel safe. The second set of skills involves blocking skills, which enable the group leader to respond to group boundary violations. Your group members aren't perfect, so boundary violations will inevitably happen over the course of your group. Nothing can derail the safety of a group more quickly than an unaddressed boundary violation. In the second part of this chapter, I discuss how you as a leader can address boundary violations when they occur.

BOUNDARY SKILLS

Boundary skills are necessary in order to create a safe group context or group container. The best approach is to make these boundaries explicit to your group members from outset. You will need to reinforce these boundaries later, but they are foundational for creating safety. Sometimes I even meet with potential group members prior to the start of group to go over the group's boundaries and expectations. Having these boundaries on a written handout that group members can sign, indicating their agreement, can also be helpful. You could even give each group member a copy of the signed agreement sheet, so that they can have a resource to remember the agreements. In the following sections, I cover each boundary and explain why it is important for group safety.

Confidentiality

Confidentiality involves keeping private the information that other group members share. A standard motto for confidentiality in groups is, "What is said in the group stays in the group." Members must know that what someone shares will not be repeated elsewhere. In my experience, when I say something to a friend and find out later that my friend shared what I said with someone else, that friend no longer feels safe. Confidentiality is essential for group safety.

Every member in the small group needs to agree to keep the boundary of confidentiality. After explaining the idea of confidentiality and why it is important, I go around to each individual in the group to make sure each person agrees. I ask for questions or aspects of the agreement that need clarification. I look each person in the eye and wait for a response.

The boundary of confidentiality has a few exceptions that group members must understand at the beginning of the group experience, so that they are not surprised if an exception occurs later in the group. Check the laws of your particular state, as well as with your supervisor, to understand clearly the limits of confidentiality for your particular small group context.

When introducing the boundary of confidentiality to the group, you might say something like this:

Confidentiality provides safety. What you hear in the group stays in the group. You can share your own work and insights with your spouse or a friend, but don't talk about the work of another group member with anyone. There are four exceptions to the rule of confidentiality that I want you to be aware of before we start. The first exception is if you were to talk about harming yourself or someone else. The second exception is if you were to report current abuse of a child or elderly person. In these situations, I would need to break confidentiality in order to keep you or the other person safe. The third exception to confidentiality is if for some reason I was required to testify in court. The fourth exception to confidentiality is my need to share some of what happens here with my own coach or supervisor. My desire is to be the best leader possible, so in order to help me be a better leader, sometime during this workshop my coach might sit in on our group experience. My coach will also agree to confidentiality. Are there any questions? I would like to go around the group and ask for each of you to commit to confidentiality.

Usually participants have no problem with the boundary of confidentiality. They understand how important it is.

How do you feel about the boundary of confidentiality? Have you addressed this issue with your group? If not, why not? Have you had any problems with group members breaking confidentiality in your group?

_____

_____

_____

No Judgments or Criticism

A second boundary that helps create safety is refraining from judging or criticizing one another. Judgments and criticism make the group feel unsafe, and members who experience a high level of judgment or criticism in the group often shut down. Think about your own life. If you are married, think of your relationship with your spouse. If you are single, think of your experience with your friendships. If you receive a lot of judgment or criticism in these relationships, does it make you want to share and open up more? Probably not. If you are like most people, judgment and criticism make you want to escape, which is not the kind of environment we want to create in our groups. In fact, we are trying to do the opposite and create an environment where people can share vulnerably about their struggles and receive grace instead of judgment. To help this happen, make it a rule that your group will be a judgment- and criticism-free zone.

This rule applies not only to your group members but also to you as the leader. Sometimes we think that we have to make judgments or criticisms in order to make group members change their behavior. This strategy doesn't usually work. Think about your own behavior as a group leader. Are you able to hold back your judgments of your group members? Are you able to stop criticizing? Make it a rule for yourself and the group. Jesus said, "Do not judge" (Matthew 7:1).

This boundary is difficult to follow. I believe this is one command Jesus gave that none of us can keep perfectly. Blaming and putting down others is a natural part of how we cope with our own brokenness and pain. Blaming is often our first response, and when we blame others, we build ourselves up and put down others. Not judging or criticizing means that we strive to always respond to others with generosity of mind and heart and a desire to strengthen the relationship. Even when we have to confront a group member, we use all the creativity and energy at our disposal to optimize the chance for growth in the relationship. We do not seek to exclude or marginalize. We do not shame or blame.

What is your reaction to "No judgments"? Are you quick to make judgments in your group? What do you do when a judgment or critical thought comes to your mind? As a leader, do you stop your group members from judging each other?

_____

_____

_____

No Advice

A third boundary that helps create safety is refraining from giving each other advice. This boundary, too, can be very difficult to follow, even for group leaders. Think about your own life. When someone comes to you for help, don't you naturally want to give the person some of your great wisdom, especially since you are a leader? Aren't you supposed to give advice? Don't do it. You cannot change your group members or anyone else, so stop giving advice. Make it a boundary, for yourself as a leader and for the group members.

Usually the motivation for giving advice comes from a good place. Your group members certainly want to give advice. They want to be helpful to each other, which is a good thing. But often something more is going on inside people when they say they want to help and give advice. For example, they may feel helpless at hearing another person's pain, and offering advice gets rid of the helpless feeling. Also, it can also make a person feel good to instruct others on how to live *their* lives. The problem is that advice-giving often sets into motion norms that undermine a thriving, vulnerable group. Instead of learning to focus on and share one's own struggles, group members increasingly focus on one or several other group members and their issues. Setting a boundary on giving advice establishes a norm that *we as a group prioritize compassionately listening and affirming vulnerability in the group and do not speed to judgment or minimize things shared in the group.* This norm helps group members look more deeply at what might really be going on inside themselves, and the truth often is that their advice is not likely to be seen as helpful. Advice does not create equal footing for group members. Instead, advice creates a context of one person being above the other, which can undermine a sense of safety. Giving advice also makes the faulty assumption that what works for one person will work for someone else.

Listen to what Jesus said following his command not to judge.

"Why do you look at the speck of sawdust in your brother's eye and pay no attention to the plank in your own eye? How can you say to your brother, 'Let me take the speck out of your eye,' when all the time there is a plank in your own eye? You hypocrite, first take the plank out of your own eye, and then you will see clearly to remove the speck from your brother's eye" (Matthew 7:3–5). It might be helpful to do some teaching around these words of Jesus and make them core to your group process.

You might say something like this to your group:

> Our second boundary is no judgments, advice giving, or attempts to fix other people in the group. We are here for one purpose, to experience healing and growth ourselves, and to become more like Christ. The best way to do that is to work on ourselves. You cannot do someone else's work for them, so resist the temptation to try to fix each other by giving advice. There is no greater way to destroy the safety of our group than to judge and criticize each other. It is so easy to judge, but I will interrupt you if that happens. Are there any questions? Can we agree to not make judgments or give advice?

You might get some pushback on the no-advice rule. For example, in my group James asked, "How can we help each other if we don't give advice?" I responded by sharing what Jesus said about judging in Matthew. Other participants may readily agree to no judgments or advice giving, but often this ground rule is quickly broken. People who are hurting readily blame others for their pain. And people like to feel better about their own lives by telling others how to live. Thus, this boundary will need to be revisited often.

Not giving advice is often a very difficult ground rule for leaders as well. It is common to think that the leader's job is to give advice. This belief is common whether you are leading a Bible or book study or a support group. Isn't your advice what others are looking for? Sometimes group members are looking for advice from the group leader, and there may be something you have to offer as you see the speck in another person's eye. We encourage you, however, to put off giving advice about participants' specks until they have done some of their own work. Invite participants to do the work on their own planks first. When participants want to give another participant advice, instead invite them to share their work on their plank. Make this a motto for the work of your group: "Planks first, specks second."

What is your reaction to "No advice"? Are you quick to give advice in your group? Do you stop your group members from giving advice to each other?

Do Your Own Work

This principle is so important that we suggest making it a fourth boundary of your group: group members *do their own work*. The group's purpose is for group members to look at the planks in their own eyes. The group is a place for people to share their bro-kenness, stories, and insights about themselves. Groups function best when everyone focuses on doing their own work.

You can model this for the group. Share openly your own story and work. We already discussed that you have your own sto-ries of brokenness, grace, and healing to share. You also have your own work available to share each week. Lead the way and then invite group members to do their work and examine their own stories—their planks. The more each person does their own work, the more each person gets out of the group experience, and the safer each person feels. Sharing one's story puts everyone on equal footing.

Doing this plank work creates a safe context and is a gift for everyone. In fact, returning to the passage in Matthew, Jesus refers to this work as sharing "pearls," and a safe group becomes a place where people's pearls are safe and honored, not "tram-pled on by pigs" (Matthew 7:6). Participants' stories of broken-ness are like pearls that need to be cared for with grace, rather than trampled on by criticism, judgments, or advice.

You as the leader might say something like:

> Instead of judgments, advice-giving, and attempting to fix each other, I'd like to encourage you to focus on your-self and do your own work. You will certainly have an opportunity to share your thoughts on any topic we will be discussing, but I want to also invite you to go deeper and share your feelings. When you say, "I feel," follow it with a feeling word, for example, "I feel sad, angry, or scared." Watch out for "I feel" statements that are actually judg-

ments—for example, "I feel that you are wrong or upset."
This is really a judgment about the other person in disguise.

What is your reaction to the boundary of "Do your own
work"? Have you made that boundary clear in your group? Do
your group members share their own planks, or are they focused
on each other's "specks"?

_____

_____

_____

Choose a Person

From the outset, express your expectations about how people
are to share. For some group members, this process is natural.
For most, however, it is more difficult. How people share (i.e.,
the process) may be more insightful than what people share (i.e.,
the content). As participants begin to share themselves and their
stories, the tendency is for them to share either to the leader or to
the group as a whole. Because I want the group to be more process oriented, I create the boundary that, as a general rule, I want
group members to be interpersonal and share with each other. I
want them to be in relationship as they do their own work, so I
ask group members to speak to each other instead of to the leader
or the group as a whole.

When a participant shares something, I invite that person to
pick another group member to be in relationship with while the

sharing takes place. Choosing another person to talk to helps make the group more interpersonal in nature. Relating to another person rather than just the leader or the group as a whole helps make this happen. For example, if I were to open the group up for someone to share, Beth might jump in. She would speak either to me or to the group as a whole. I would stop her and ask her to pick another group member to be in relationship with as she shared. I would explain that, "We all will be involved, but since I believe that healing happens through relationships, and because my story is that we could use some help with our relationships, I want to help make relationships happen in this group. One way to do that is to have you practice talking to each other. So, Beth, I want you to pick another person. Then I will invite that person to respond to what you have to say. And then I will open it up for others in the group to respond." By setting this boundary, I create a group that is increasingly more process oriented and relational in nature. After one person shares with another person, both people have the opportunity to give each other feedback on their interaction with each other.

This may be a new boundary for you as a leader to consider. What is your reaction to asking group members to talk to each other? What is your experience with your group? Do group members speak to you, the leader; to the group as a whole; or to each other? Might you want to add this boundary with your group?

Okay to Pass; Do Not Dominate

To feel safe, participants need to be free to talk (or not talk) in the small group, especially at the beginning. To make this happen, the quieter participants need to feel free to pass. Quiet participants often report that they are getting a lot out of what the others are saying. A motto that I often repeat in small groups is, "When one person works, everyone works." So, those who are quiet are indeed working. Research does indicate, however, that those who more actively participate get more out of the group work (Yalom, 1970), so while it is helpful to encourage the quieter group members to stretch themselves and participate verbally, don't force them to do so.

The silence of group members is often a sign that they are afraid to share. Fear is natural, and I invite participants to step into their fear, face the scary feelings they experience, and share as much as possible. I believe that the more vulnerable a person can be, and the more a person can share their own heart, the more healing that person will experience, as long as the group is safe. Members, though, should still have the option to pass.

Groups have introverts, people like Jane and James, who are naturally more quiet. They often have much to contribute and need to be invited. I periodically invite the silent members to share their thoughts and feelings. I don't ask just once, but periodically throughout the session I invite the quieter members to share. As the group experiences the terrain as increasingly safe, the quieter individuals tend to gradually increase their sharing. If the silent members never share, you need to address their silence later in the life of the group. But at the beginning, invite and be okay with group members who choose to pass.

On the other hand, do not let any one member dominate the discussion. Small groups also have extroverts—people like Edward, Ted, and Beth. They tend to talk a lot when they share, and if you let them talk for too long, they disrupt the group's safety. You might want to set a time limit; for example, make a boundary of three minutes of sharing per person. Time limits allow everyone to have the opportunity to share, and this boundary can increase safety. If making a time limit sounds too rigid for you, then use your intuition as a guide. As you gain more experience leading small groups, you will sense when someone is going on too long. Tell the group members at the beginning that you will stop a person who talks too long. Establishing this norm early in the group's life gives you greater permission to interrupt a dominating group member as the group progresses. Then make sure you follow through on your boundary. There may be times when you want to break this boundary (e.g., spending extra time helping a group member who is in crisis), but as a general rule, giving time for everyone makes a group safe.

You might say something like this:

> Another boundary is to not dominate the group time. I am going to ask that you try to keep your sharing to around three minutes so that everyone gets a chance to share. If your sharing goes on too long, I will gently remind you that we need to move on so that someone else can speak. On the other hand, no one has to share. It will be each person's choice how much to share, but my hope is that you will all share at whatever level you are comfortable. We are here to learn from each other. Each of you has a valuable contribu-

tion to the group's growth process, and my experience tells me that the more you put into this group, the more you will get out of the experience. If you are silent, I will invite you to share, but you can choose to not share if you wish.

What is your reaction to this boundary? If you are already more process oriented in your leading, you may think that holding this boundary is too controlling. Perhaps try letting the talker go on for a while and see how the group responds. Be aware of how you are feeling about someone talking so long. If it is early in the group process, you may need to jump in and check out others' reactions to the person talking so long. As the group becomes safe over time, you might want to wait and see what happens. See if someone else jumps in or confronts the talker. The same could be true for the silent person. You might let the silence go and see how others react to the person not talking. After safety has been established, I typically let this happen. Initially, however, I take more control, stop the talker, and invite the nontalker. What are your thoughts on these suggested boundaries?

_____

_____

_____

Commit to Attend

The final boundary is for members to commit to come to each scheduled group session. Consistency helps create safety. As group members see the same people over time and experience the ground rules in action, they feel safe. Whenever a person skips group, not only does the person miss out on what has happened in the group, but the other participants in the small group also miss out. Each person is vital to the group's healing and growth process.

The Bible says, "Let us consider how we may spur one another on toward love and good deeds, not giving up meeting together, as some are in the habit of doing, but encouraging one another" (Hebrews 10:24–25). As people commit to attending group on a regular basis, the sense of safety grows and participants are increasingly able to give and receive encouragement. People count on each other's presence.

Unfortunately, commitment is a challenge for many small groups. People often do not follow through on their promises. Making consistent attendance a boundary at the beginning of group and following through on the boundary are important elements of keeping the group safe. Leaders and group members both have a much more positive experience in groups that are fully committed compared to groups that are not fully committed.

I encourage members to let the group know if they are going to be absent the following session. If something comes up between sessions, I have group members let the leader know that they will be absent. Letting the group know of absences shows respect, and continuity and safety are more likely to be maintained.

You might say something like:

> In order for this group to work most effectively, we all need
> to commit to being here, regularly, every week. That may

be difficult. There may be times when you are out of town, or when this group is the last place you want to be. I know that I will be here. If you know that you will be absent, let the group know, and if something comes up that will cause you to miss, give me a call and let me know, so I can keep the group in the loop. How about the rest of you? Can you commit to this?

Go around the group and ask about each person's level of commitment to the group. If some group members are not able to commit to consistent attendance, they may not be good group candidates.

I am fortunate that, as a professional therapist, I can charge my clients for group whether they show up or not. This enhances the probability that everyone attends. However, I often find consistent attendance more difficult to address in other types of groups (e.g., church or support groups), so for them I make a big deal about a commitment to consistent group attendance. I have had group members put their commitments in writing. The more consistent group members are in attending, the safer the group is.

What is your experience around the commitment to meet in the small groups that you lead? How difficult has this been for participants? What works for you? Might you need to make commitment a more important boundary with your group members?

Setting Up Boundaries

Healing and growth take place in the context of safe relationships. Because of this, I want to encourage you to work very hard at creating a safe group context. These boundaries are necessary to create safety. State them early in the group process and reinforce them as needed. Make these boundaries apply not only to the small group but to individuals as they relate to each other, even when they are outside the small group.

Ideally, you want to set up these boundaries from the very beginning of the group. Some of you, however, may already be in the middle of leading a small group and you recognize that you need to apply some of these boundaries now. What do you do if some of these boundary violations are already happening in your small group?

If you do not have all these boundaries in place, add them now in order to create more safety. Be transparent. Tell your group that you are reading this book and want to experiment with some ways to make the group a safer place. If these boundaries are already being violated, some members in the group are probably not feeling safe, and a different way of doing group would be welcomed. Explain all the boundaries to group members rather than just the one rule that you think applies. In this way, you are not focusing on one particular problem. Go through all the ground rules and begin to enforce them. Experiment and see what happens.

Exercise: Where Are You Right Now?

As you reflect on the ground rules that help to create safety, can you commit to these boundaries? What would get in the way?

Write about your reservations and talk about them with other leaders. It is okay to be skeptical, but I want to encourage you to give these boundaries a try. Experiment with them. Try them out for the time it takes to work through the book. If you have already been leading your group, assess yourself. Which of these boundaries are you already using? Which boundaries do you need to add? Consider bringing all these boundaries to your group in order to create a safer environment. Which of these boundaries are you good at? Which of these boundaries are difficult for you? Pick one to work on the next time you meet with your group.

BLOCKING SKILLS

Even if you do a good job of setting up the group's boundaries at the beginning, members eventually test and violate the limits. Your group members are not perfect, and they will not be able to adhere to the boundaries at all times. For example, when group members share, judgments lay right beneath the surface. Instead of listening, group members criticize each other and give advice. Group members won't show up to group even when they have made a commitment. They break established boundaries, and it takes leadership on your part to reinforce the boundaries that you have created. The challenge for you as a group leader is to keep the group safe as you encounter boundary violations from group members. At this point, you need blocking skills.

Very important for a successful group experience, blocking skills reinforce the boundaries that you have set up at the beginning of the group and help keep the group safe. Nothing damages the safety of the group more quickly than letting a boundary violation go without stopping or blocking it. Group members may agree to not judge or criticize, and to do their own work, but the first thing many hurting group members do is criticize, dominate, and give advice to others. These boundary violations need to be blocked to maintain safety in your group. Group members think that if you would let criticism go with one person, then you would let it go if they are criticized, which leads to group members shutting down and not sharing.

Let's go back to the example at the beginning of the chapter. Two boundary violations happened in this dialogue. First, Alice was struggling to do her own work. Instead, she was sharing her intellectual understanding of the story and how the story applied to other people in her life. Second, Edward judged Alice by saying, "Alice, can't you see that you're doing it again? You're going on and on, but you aren't really doing any real work. Stop giving us a sermon and share something about yourself." How I handle this second boundary violation in particular is very important. If I let it slide, Alice might either attack back or withdraw and not talk again in the group. She might even quit the group altogether. Other members would also be waiting to see what I do. If I don't do anything, they might also be afraid to share because Edward might judge them, too. I need to intervene in order to maintain safety.

Put yourself into the leader role for a minute and think back on your group experience. What if this interaction surfaced in your group? How have you responded when one group member criticized another? What did you feel? What did you do?

Intervening can be a difficult skill for group members to develop. Group leaders often struggle to bring up issues that members might view as confrontational. Group leaders might worry that if they confront a member for a boundary violation, the group member who was confronted might feel bad or even quit the group. My view is that intervening to block a boundary violation is one of the most important skills to develop as a group leader if you want to maintain safety in your group. Furthermore, blocking boundary violations may even help your group members because it models how to engage in confrontation and conflict in a healthy and balanced manner. To block boundary violations when they occur, I recommend following the I-R-R (Interrupt-Reinforce-Redirect) model.

Interrupt

When a boundary violation occurs, the first blocking skill is to interrupt the process and identify the violation. Say something like, "Edward, I want to interrupt you," or, "Edward, I need you to stop." After interrupting, I paraphrase what the violator said to make sure I heard him right, and I identify what he said as a boundary violation. I get as close to the content as possible, maybe repeating his comments verbatim.

Interrupting is not easy to do, especially for beginning group leaders who want group members to like them. New leaders who interrupt might be afraid that participants will be angry, but these new leaders need to work through their desire for acceptance. Your group members depend on you more importantly to create a safe environment, where boundaries are not easily or lightly violated.

Another issue that might get in the way of interrupting a boundary violation is fear of conflict. Again, in order to keep the group safe, leaders need to be able to work through any fears about creating conflict. Be aware of your feelings and experiences around conflict and how they might get in the way of you blocking boundary violations.

For me, interrupting boundary violations has been challenging. I felt fear when I interrupted Edward. I wondered how he might respond to my stopping him and challenging him with a boundary violation. I was afraid he might get angry and not like me as a leader. Yet, if I did not interrupt, I knew that group safety was at stake. I needed to interrupt and risk the chance that conflict might happen.

If you do not interrupt, not only does the group begin to feel unsafe for others, but it takes more work to heal any hurt that may have happened because of the boundary violation. For example, if I had not interrupted and confronted Edward's criticism, Alice probably would have experienced being hurt. Her response may have been either to attack back, which meant I would have had a fight on my hands, or withdraw, which meant I would have had to work very hard to help Alice recover from the hurt in order to participate in group again. So, the first step is to interrupt quickly and frequently with boundary violations, especially early on in the group's life.

Another time you need to interrupt often is if you are adding a new boundary to your group and you want that new boundary to quickly become part of the group culture. For example, maybe someone is dominating and you set a new boundary of not dominating. You need to interrupt often as you add this new boundary to your group. Face your fear and trust that, as you set the boundaries and reinforce them, you are creating a safe group where healing and growth can happen.

Reinforce

After interrupting the group member who is violating a boundary, the second blocking skill is to reinforce the boundary, which means reminding the group member and the rest of the group of the boundary that was violated. Repeat the boundary rule and remind members that you interrupt when boundaries are violated. For example, after interrupting Edward's criticism, I might say, "Remember the boundaries that we agreed upon. We agreed to not judge and criticize each other. The reason we have this boundary is to keep the group safe." You may use the reinforcing of one boundary as an opportunity to remind the group members of the other boundaries. These reminders reinforce the other boundaries, too.

Redirect

After you have interrupted the violation and reinforced the boundary, the final blocking skill is to redirect the boundary violation. Redirecting the boundary violation is the process of bringing the violator back to the group's goal, which is to do one's own work, exploring and working on the planks that are in each of our eyes. Invite the boundary violator to own the violation and do some work about what the boundary violation is about for them. For example, I might say, "So, Edward, you are making a judgment about Alice when you say she isn't doing any real work. Remember that instead of making a judgment, our commitment in this group is to work on our planks. Can you say what that criticism was about for you? What are feeling when you say that? What is the story you are making up about that?"

You may need to help group members unpack the story behind the judgments they make. But right now, in the forming stage of group, it may be enough to interrupt the boundary violation, reinforce the boundary, and invite the violator to look at what is behind a particular violation—that is, to look at the plank in their own eye and move on. When I asked Edward what the criticism was about for him, he replied, "I don't know." At this early point in the group process, I did not push him to explore further but simply invited him to explore his plank first. I asked if he would be open to that. He said, "Yes," and we moved on.

Another common example that needs to be blocked and redirected is when one person speaks for someone else in the group. For example, in my group Jane tried to smooth things over and said, "Oh, Edward is just trying to help." At that point, I need to interrupt, reinforce, and redirect. I could say something like,

"Jane, right now you are speaking for Edward. Again, I want to invite you and everyone in the group to work on speaking for yourselves. Jane, you sounded like you want to support Edward when you said, 'He's just trying to help.' However, when you did that, you were speaking for him, and I want to invite you to work on speaking for yourself." If I wanted to pursue Jane further, I might ask her, "Can you share what was going on inside you when Edward made the judgment?" Early in the group process, however, I might just reinforce the boundary and move on.

Redirecting puts the responsibility for the boundary violation back on the person breaking the boundary. Hopefully the violator gains insight through exploring what underlies the violation. And when the victim hears the offender own the boundary violation, the victim may feel less attacked and hurt. Victims see that it is the violator's problem and not theirs, and they won't need to be defensive. Make sure to follow up with the violator as well, though, to explore how it feels to be on that side of the exchange.

When I asked Edward, "What is that about for you?" my question opened the door for Edward to at least think about his plank. Also, by addressing Edward and encouraging him to do his own work, my hope is that Alice and other group members feel safe as a result, knowing that the boundary violation was addressed. Alice will likely feel less of a need to defend herself going forward as she experiences Edward working on his own issues. Other group members who experience my intervention may be more likely to share, knowing that I keep the group safe and do not let members judge and criticize others. Group members also begin to understand where Edward's criticism is coming from as Edward does his work. Group members may even begin to have compassion for Edward's struggle with criticism and not be scared or angered by him. Interrupting, reinforcing, and redirecting when boundaries are violated create excellent opportunities for growth to happen in your small group. Doing this kind of work moves the group toward a process of interpersonal healing.

SAFETY EXERCISE: INDIVIDUAL

Take some time to reflect on the boundary and blocking skills that create safety in your small group. Which boundary skills have you included in your group already? Which boundary skills have you not yet included? Which boundary skills do you feel comfortable or not as comfortable with in your group? Which boundary skills do you manage well or not so well in your own life? Moving forward, what would you like to change about your group and its boundary skills?

_____

_____

_____

What happens in your group when a boundary is broken? How do you respond as the group leader? Do you interrupt, reinforce, and redirect? Which blocking skills have you included in your group already? Which skills have you not yet included in your group? Which blocking skills do you feel comfortable or not as comfortable with in your group? When someone crosses a boundary in your own life, what is your tendency? How are you at naming your own boundaries and confronting boundary violations in your own life? Moving forward, what would you like to change about your group regarding its blocking skills?

_____

_____

_____

Reflect on your ability to explain and set up the boundaries in your group, as well your ability to block boundary violations when they inevitably occur. Which of these skills do you do well or not so well? Pick a skill and commit to practicing it. Write down your growth edge for safety.

_____

_____

_____

SAFETY EXERCISE: GROUP

If you are working through this book as part of training with other readers, complete a group exercise focused on boundary and blocking skills.

The first exercise involves explaining the boundaries in a small group setting. In your group, take turns being the leader. The first person picks one of the boundaries and practices explaining the boundary to the group. Group members can ask questions for clarification, and the leader can practice answering these types of questions. When complete, ask the group for feedback. What was the explanation of the boundary like? What parts of the explanation were clear? What parts of the explanation were less clear? Did the group leader appear comfortable explaining the boundary, answering questions, and giving clarification? How could the leader improve? Once this process is finished, repeat the process with each person in the group practicing being the leader and explaining a different boundary.

The second exercise involves blocking a boundary violation. Again, in your group, take turns playing each of the roles. First, one person acts as the leader, a second person shares something with the group, and a third person plays the role of the boundary violator. (Try to share something real, but not something that is extremely personal. The idea is to practice boundary violations, and it does not feel good to be judged or criticized for something deeply personal, even in practice.) The leader jumps in and practices reinforcing the boundary of picking someone to share with. The second person picks someone to share with and shares something with that person. The boundary violator responds to the sharing with judgment, criticism, or advice giving. The leader then practices blocking the boundary violation by interrupting, reinforcing, and redirecting. After this is finished, ask the group for feedback. Did the group leader jump in right away or let the judgment or criticism go on too long? Was the explanation of the boundary violation clear? Was the group leader able to confront the violation without shaming the group member who made it? Did the group leader redirect the group member who made the boundary violation to examine what was behind the judgment, criticism, or advice? How could the leader improve? Once this process is complete, repeat the process with each person in the group practicing being the leader and blocking a boundary violation.

Vulnerability

VULNERABILITY, THE THIRD step of The Healing Cycle, involves sharing ourselves openly and honestly. When we are vulnerable, we open ourselves up for others to see us as we truly are. All of us wear masks in which we put forth a certain image. Vulnerability involves taking off our masks and allowing others to see us in a real, exposed way. We do this by giving people access to our experiences, thoughts, and feelings. It allows others to see the unedited self, including the good, the bad, and the ugly.

Vulnerability is important because healing and growth occur in your small group as your group members bring problematic aspects of their lives out into the open and work through them in relationship with other group members. This growth process is both beautiful and messy. When group members conceal their true selves from each other, this process never has a chance to succeed.

Groups have various levels of vulnerability. At the most superficial level (Level 1), group members do not talk about themselves or their experiences. Instead, group members talk about a topic or event rather than sharing their personal experiences with it. This level is common, especially for beginning group members. At the next level of sharing (Level 2), group members talk about the personal experience of *other people*. They share about real issues, but the issues may be those of other group members or their family members outside of group. At these first two levels of sharing, group members are not yet talking about themselves.

At the next level of sharing (Level 3), group members share about their own personal experiences. This type of sharing can be deep and vulnerable, especially if it involves painful experiences of hurt or even trauma. At the next level of sharing (Level 4), group members share their thoughts and beliefs about themselves. This type of sharing can also be deep and vulnerable, especially if it involves difficult core beliefs (e.g., a group member who believes that they are unworthy of love). At the deepest level of sharing (Level 5), group members share their feelings and emotions. In my groups, I often use the acronym SASHET (i.e., sad, angry, scared, happy, excited, tender; Morris & Morris, 1985) to help people name their emotions. Feelings and emotions can be especially deep and vulnerable and are a key way that your group members connect with each other on a heart level.

PSYCHOLOGY AND VULNERABILITY

Vulnerability is often a key component to effective counseling. In many forms of counseling, clients are encouraged to share whatever comes to their mind, including their deepest thoughts and feelings (e.g., free association [Jones, 1963]). Clients are encouraged to share and discuss without the normal filter that they would use in their everyday lives. The idea is that by sharing vulnerably, the counselor and the client are able to discuss and work through what is really going on in the client's heart and mind, without having to worry about what is said. In this vulnerable place, true healing and change can occur.

We discussed Yalom earlier, one of the pioneers of group therapy (Yalom, 1970). He noted vulnerability as one of the key factors in forming group cohesion, which he viewed as perhaps the fundamental element of all effective groups (Tschuschke & Dies, 1994). Although definitions are multifaceted (Carron & Brawley, 2000), at its core, cohesion is the degree to which a group develops a sense of we-ness. Vulnerable sharing also releases a variety of other therapeutic factors. Group members change as they experience catharsis—emotional release—combined with insight. In addition, sharing vulnerably with each other helps group members realize that other people deal with similar pain and struggles. Other researchers, such as Brene Brown (2012), have posited that vulnerability is key to healing and working through shame.

CHRISTIANITY AND VULNERABILITY

True Christian faith involves vulnerability across one's relationships. In the Genesis narrative (Genesis 1–3), God's original plan was for humans to be completely vulnerable, both with God and with one another. For example, Adam walked with God in the cool of the garden, experiencing true intimacy. Adam and Eve engaged with each other from a place of true vulnerability, being "naked and unashamed." In the Genesis narrative, sin involves a loss of vulnerability. Hiding replaced vulnerability. Adam and Eve hid from God. Instead of walking in the garden in true intimacy, God had to search for Adam and Eve. Adam and Eve also hid from each other. Instead of being naked and unashamed, Adam and Eve realized they were naked and sewed fig leaves together to cover themselves, creating separation from each other.

God is working throughout history to redeem creation. Restoring vulnerability and intimacy is a fundamental aspect of God's redemptive plan. For example, the Psalms are full of examples of individuals pouring their heart out to God. In Psalm 6, David expresses his deepest struggles and pain to God: "Have mercy on me, LORD, for I am faint; heal me, LORD, for my bones are in agony. My soul is in deep anguish. How long, LORD, how long? . . . I am worn out from my groaning. All night long I flood my bed with weeping and drench my couch with tears" (Psalm 6:2–3, 6). David doesn't hold back with God or conceal aspects of his heart. Instead, he shares the deepest parts of himself, including the difficult and painful parts.

In a similar way, true Christian community involves vulnerable sharing and carrying one another's burdens. In Luke 7, a sinful woman displays vulnerability when she kneels before the feet of Jesus, pours a jar of ointment at his feet, wets his feet with her tears, and wipes his feet with her hair. Jesus blesses her vulnerability, forgiving her sins and telling her to go in peace. When he gave instructions to the church in Galatia, Paul wrote, "Carry each other's burdens, and in this way you will fulfill the law of Christ" (Galatians 6:2). In this passage, Paul connects vulnerability and carrying each others' burdens with love, which is the law of Christ. True love requires vulnerability. In his book *The Four Loves*, C. S. Lewis (1960) highlights this connection between vulnerability and love:

To love at all is to be vulnerable. Love anything, and your heart will certainly be wrung and possibly be broken. If you want to make sure of keeping it intact, you must give your heart to no one, not even to an animal. Wrap it carefully round with hobbies and little luxuries; avoid all entanglements; lock it up safe in the casket or coffin of your selfishness. But in that casket—safe, dark, motionless, airless—it will change. It will not be broken; it will become unbreakable, impenetrable, irredeemable. The alternative to tragedy is damnation. The only place outside of heaven where you can be perfectly safe from all the dangers and perturbations of love is hell.

God's plan is for us to be vulnerable with one another. Vulnerability is necessary for a loving, supportive community to flourish. It allows us to give and receive love, and carry each others' burdens. Vulnerability is an important prerequisite for any type of meaningful healing and growth to occur. Thus, you must make vulnerability a foundational part of your small group.

STRUGGLING WITH VULNERABILITY IN THE GROUP

I was excited about this small group session. My plan was to have the group reflect on Ephesians 4:15, which focuses on the importance of speaking the truth in love. For a while, I had been feeling that my group members struggled with this tension and balance. It seemed like some of the group members focused more on truth, but they communicated their truth in an unloving way, blasting their family members and friends. Others seemed to be more focused on love. They were good at loving their family members and friends, but had trouble setting boundaries, which resulted in others taking advantage of them. I had the sense my group members struggled to integrate truth and love in their own lives as well. Some members struggled to give themselves grace, hurting themselves with the "truth" of their limitations and struggles. Others struggled to acknowledge the "truth" about how their actions were hurting themselves and others. I was excited about the possibilities of using this passage to initiate vulnerable sharing among my group members.

I started the session by reading the passage out loud a few times, inviting the group members to close their eyes, listen, and reflect on the passage. This is a practice known as *lectio divina*, an ancient process used to help people meditate on scripture. I invited each of the group members to land on a particular word or phrase that touched them and to let God speak to them around that word or phrase. After giving them some time to meditate, I invited them to share, asking, "What was God saying to you?" I looked around the group, eagerly anticipating what would happen.

Unfortunately, the sharing didn't quite go as I had hoped. At first, there was silence, as if each of the group members were waiting for someone else to talk. The silence went on for a while, and I started to feel uncomfortable and anxious. How long was the silence going to last? Was anyone going to share? Finally, James broke the ice. At first, I felt relief. I also felt excited, because James had a tendency to be quiet and not participate much in group. As James talked, however, I started to feel frustrated. James began to share about how there wasn't enough truth-telling in politics nowadays. While there might have been some facts in what he said, his sharing wasn't very vulnerable. It wasn't even about him.

Jane jumped in and agreed with James about the state of politics in the United States. She began to talk about the national media, and how they only report one viewpoint about issues. Speaking the truth in love meant giving equal time to both sides of a particular issue. Beth jumped in and said that she also thought a lot of the discussion in the media wasn't said with a very loving tone either, just people arguing back and forth.

The conversation went on for a while, and I wasn't quite sure how to feel. At least the group members were talking and sharing their opinions, which felt better than silence. And they were on topic—they were discussing the idea of speaking the truth in love. But something still didn't seem right. Even though the group members were talking about the topic, they weren't sharing with much vulnerability. The conversation was mostly superficial. The group members were talking *about* speaking the truth in love, rather than sharing how *they personally engaged* with speaking the truth in love, or *struggled* to speak the truth in love in their own lives.

This is a common issue when leading small groups. Group members often resist sharing vulnerably about themselves, even if you have done a good job creating an atmosphere of grace and safety in your small group. Without intentional direction by the leader, group members often stay on the surface, talking about a particular topic rather than sharing their personal experience with the topic. Another common way that group members avoid sharing vulnerably is to focus on the experiences of other people.

Group members might share about a problem one of their family members or friends is having, rather than sharing their own struggles or concerns. Or they might focus on what is happening with other group members, rather than doing their own work. They may discuss or debate ideas in the abstract—even about very intimate topics—but all of their talking does not reveal much about themselves. Some group members might just remain silent. These various strategies all work toward the same end: they maintain a safe distance from being close to others, protecting them from the potential for disappointment and betrayal.

Before I begin exploring how to encourage vulnerability in your small group members, I would like you to remember how it felt to think about sharing your story of brokenness in a group of people you didn't know well. In regular life, we generally don't share vulnerably with others until we know them very well. Sometimes we might never share vulnerably with another person. I think the reason we don't share vulnerably is because of the risk. What if we share some really deep stuff and get rejected? What if we show our true selves and aren't accepted? That would feel terrible. As group leaders, we can do our best to create contexts of grace and safety, but the truth is that it is still a risk for group members to share vulnerably. Being close to others stirs deep spiritual desires for love and belonging. Some writers have referred to this as a homesickness for Eden (Moon, 1997). We cannot possibly prevent group members from feeling hurt or pain when their actual relationships with group members fall short of these longings for Eden. These longings also stir up group members' habits of trying to ease the pain of not feeling fully loved and safe.

Even though vulnerability is difficult, it is an essential ingredient for healing and growth to happen in your small group. Thus, the purpose of this chapter is to help you help your group members share vulnerably with each other. As you aid group members in sharing more of their story in a deeper way, a context is created for healing and growth to happen. Members begin to stop blaming others and become more open to explore their own areas of brokenness. Their walls and defenses begin to soften.

Reflect back on your healing process. Do you remember a time when you felt safe enough to share more deeply? What about the context or relationship made it feel safe to share vulnerably? How important was that to your healing process?

_____

_____

_____

I will never forget the experience I had when I shared vulnerably with one of my work colleagues. During my time of struggle when my son was experiencing health problems, I shared with him what I was going through. He had gone through a similar experience with his son. He had been through some healing and could understand my struggle. He was safe and offered me grace. As a result, I was able to share even more of my story. I was able to go deeper and express my anger, fear, and confusion. I was able to share more vulnerably, and his response made me feel heard and understood. This was a huge step in my healing process.

Encouraging Vulnerability

As you lead with an attitude of grace and create a safe place in your group, group members will likely begin to share more vulnerably. Still, vulnerability is difficult and scary. As a group leader, you can develop some skills to help your group members share more vulnerably. The four sets of skills I discuss are (a) listening skills, (b) facilitating skills, (c) linking skills, and (d) self-disclosure skills. These skills build on the grace and safety skills discussed previously.

Listening Skills

The first and most important way to promote vulnerability in your group involves listening well. When group members share, they need to be listened to and heard. Listening skills are necessary for members to feel comfortable going into deeper levels of vulnerability. Listening skills are also important to help group members connect with each other. Accordingly, as the leader, you can establish norms by consistently modeling good listening skills. Your goal is to listen to the group members well and invite them to listen to each other. Listening is the most basic way to love, honors someone in the highest way, and is key to the healing process. There are three important listening skills to develop as a group leader: SOLER, paraphrasing, and summarizing.

SOLER

SOLER is an acronym to help you to remember to listen well (Egan, 1986). The letters stand for

Squarely
Open
Lean Forward
Eye Contact
Relaxed

Make sure that you practice SOLER as described here so that it comes naturally when you lead your group.

First, face your participants *squarely* when you listen. Facing squarely shows that you are focused on the person who is sharing. Turning away from the speaker can communicate disinterest and disrespect. Second, be *open* with your body posture. Uncross your arms and legs. Third, *lean forward*. Leaning forward toward the person who is sharing communicates that you are interested in and engaged with what the speaker is saying. Fourth, make *eye contact* with the person who is sharing. Making eye contact helps promote connection, while looking away can communicate disinterest. Fifth, be *relaxed*. Being relaxed is key, especially for beginning leaders. It is easy to try too hard to be present and communicate too intensely as you work at being present. Relax as you practice and model these skills. Following the SOLER guidelines demonstrates that you are physically present with your participants and helps create safety in your group. Help your group members develop their listening skills by inviting them to follow the SOLER guidelines as well. In addition, make group members aware when you see them violating the SOLER guidelines, which hurts their presence to the group.

When members practice the SOLER guidelines, this positively affects the group process. For example, James is one of the quieter group members. I keep wanting to invite him to share more. However, I often notice that, even though he is silent, he seems to be physically present. To affirm him for being present and listening well, I might say, "James, even though you have been quiet, I really like how present you seem today. Your body is leaning forward and your eyes are really tuned into the interaction that is going on." Sometimes I challenge group members who are not being fully present. For example, I might say, "Alice, I notice that your body is turning away and your eyes are looking down as Ted is talking. I want to invite you to open up and look at him as he is talking." Listening physically using SOLER is the first step to listening effectively.

Paraphrasing

After learning to listen bodily using SOLER, the next important listening skill is paraphrasing. Paraphrasing involves reflecting back in your own words what the group members are sharing (Egan, 1986). It is important for group members not only to be heard but also to know that others understand the content of what is being shared. Paraphrasing shows your group members that you are getting the gist of what is being said. Begin your paraphrase by saying, "What I hear you saying is . . . ," and then reflect back what you hear. Work hard at getting the gist of what is said and not just parroting back what you hear word for word. Then say, "Did I get that right?" Paraphrasing is especially important when a group member shares something confusing. Paraphrasing will help you to get it right, and as you do the group members feel understood.

Let's go back to the example from earlier in the chapter. When responding to the meditation on the Bible verse, "Instead, speaking the truth in love we will in all things grow up into him who is the Head, that is, Christ," I invited the group to switch gears from talking about politics and instead share something more personal. James shared about an exchange he had at work: "I had to reprimand one of my colleagues last week because he was not doing his job right. He needed to hear some truth. So I told him off, but it was for his own good. I spoke the truth in love by telling him he wasn't doing his job right."

When I heard James share, the thought that popped into my head was, *How was this response an example of speaking the truth in love? It didn't sound particularly loving to me.* One response could be to ask James that question, but another option would be to paraphrase James's statement to let him know I was really listening to him. How might you paraphrase James? Write down your paraphrase.

I paraphrased by saying, "I hear you saying that you challenged a colleague because he wasn't doing a good job. It sounds like you thought that your challenge was a loving thing to do. Is that right?"

He said, "Yes, that's right." By paraphrasing, I am trying to make sure that I understand the content of what James is saying. My hope is that James experiences me hearing him, and that he feels safe and responds by sharing more. Others in the group will also experience me working on listening and think that if they share something personal, I will listen to them. Paraphrasing shows that I am really listening and working at getting correct the content of what is said.

Another benefit of paraphrasing is that, as you paraphrase back what you heard, you help the sharer hear and potentially clarify what was shared. For example, after being paraphrased the group member might say, "Oh, I didn't really mean that. What I really mean to say is _____." Thus, paraphrasing provides an opportunity for understanding and clarification.

This is what happened with James. After he said, "You have it right," I paraphrased again, emphasizing how strongly he told off his colleague and contrasting that with him thinking he was being loving.

I said, "James, when you said, 'I told him off and it was for his own good,' you were also saying that you were really being loving."

My paraphrase caused James to think more about what he said, and he responded with a smile. "Well, maybe that doesn't sound quite so loving." The paraphrasing gave him a chance to self-reflect on what was really going on, and he had a chance to restate what he really wanted to say.

Notice the example given above regarding James and my paraphrasing him. This is an important part of effective listening, but the interaction is between the group member and group leader. As the group progresses, I look for the group to be more interactive with one another and not have all the dialogue going through me as the group leader. I also do much less paraphrasing in group than I do in individual counseling, listening more without paraphrasing. I tend to only jump in and paraphrase if the sharing is confusing. Also, I invite others to paraphrase if what I hear sounds confusing. I might say to the group, "What do you hear James saying?" When someone paraphrases, I have that person talk directly to James. "Can you say that to James?" This approach makes the group more interactive and interpersonal.

Summarizing

Summarizing is similar to paraphrasing, except it involves putting together several ideas or transactions that have happened in the group (Egan, 1986). You might summarize when finishing a time of teaching in order to transition the group into discussion time, when transitioning between topics covered during group time or at the end of group time, or to address some of the interactions that have happened in group.

Summarizing helps tie things together and lets participants know that you have been hearing what has been said. As such, summarizing can create a nice transition to your next intervention as a leader. For example, in dealing with the previous transactions, I might summarize by saying, "James said how he applied 'speaking the truth in love' to his work situation. What about someone else? How did you apply the passage?" Summarizing helps participants reflect on what has happened during group time and can be a great way to end your group.

One helpful exercise is for group members to summarize what they have received from the group experience. This could be done as a checkout at the end of group time, with participants taking just one minute to share their feelings. Use SASHET (sad, angry, scared, happy, excited, tender), and have the members summarize what they did or did not get out of the group experience. It is so important for group members to feel heard and listened to. Being truly heard is probably the closest thing to experiencing grace in your small group. The more your group members experience being truly heard, the deeper and more vulnerably they will share.

FACILITATING SKILLS

Facilitating skills reinforce and encourage group members to continue sharing their story in a deeper and more vulnerable way. Three important facilitating skills to develop as a group leader are validation, empathy, and clarification.

Validation

When group members share, they need to be validated, which means conveying not only that you understand what they said but also that you accept and affirm their feelings and current experience. Feeling validated is like taking a breath after being under water for a while. People need to know that what they are saying makes sense and is valued. Group members will be nervous when sharing their stories. They will wonder what others think of them, especially you as the leader. Group members fear being judged, and this fear is especially poignant when they are hurting. They are trying to cope with their pain and often wonder if they are acting "crazy" in how they are trying to cope. It is your job as group leader to make sense of what they are sharing. As what they say begins to make sense, you need to validate what they are saying, so that the participant who is hurting gets affirmed.

You don't need to say much in order to validate. After a group member shares, you can say phrases like, "Thanks for sharing," or "It took a lot of courage to share that." When you really understand what has been said, you can say, "That makes sense to me" and paraphrase what they said that made sense. For example, in order to validate what James said to the group, after paraphrasing, I might say, "Thanks for sharing James. I really like it that you are personally applying the scripture to your work situation."

Validation is important for continued safety. Participants need to get that their responses are important and worth sharing and receiving. If participants are validated, there is a good chance that they will continue to share. If James is to go deeper with his sharing, he needs to continue to feel safe. Validating helps continue to create a safe container in which group members can share more and more deeply.

Empathy

After validation, empathy is an essential facilitating skill that involves reflecting back the feelings that were shared and understanding at a deeper level. Empathy helps group members experience being understood at the heart level. You can think of paraphrasing as addressing the content at the head level, whereas empathy gets to the heart. When you are accurate with your empathy, you often get a strong "yes" response, and group members want to share more often and deeply. Everyone longs to be understood at a heart level, and empathy is essential for that understanding to happen. "The purposes of a person's heart are deep waters, but one who has insight draws them out" (Proverbs 20:5–6). Empathize by saying, "It sounds like you feel [SASHET; sad, angry, scared, happy, excited, tender] because _____."

The key to empathy is connecting the content of what was said (i.e., paraphrasing) with the emotions underneath the content. Empathy requires listening with a heart of compassion. Ask yourself, "What would it be like to be in that person's shoes and experiencing what that person is experiencing?" Then share your empathy. Jesus modeled empathy by becoming human and entering into our world, so that he could truly experience what we experience. He communicated empathy with those he came in contact with and continues to empathize with us. The author of Hebrews wrote about Jesus, "For we do not have a high priest who is unable to sympathize with our weaknesses, but we have one who has been tempted in every way, just as we are" (Hebrews 4:15).

I encourage you to practice empathy. Your group members long to be understood. Your empathy will help them feel understood, and they will want to share more and share more deeply. Sometimes expressing empathy can be difficult. Most of us didn't grow up learning to empathize, but empathy gets easier with practice. Importantly, empathy is not repeating or parroting what was said, but sharing the gist of what is heard and then sharing the feeling that you are hearing. If someone is feeling sad, angry, scared, happy, excited, or tender, and you can reflect back to them what they are feeling, they will feel understood.

Continuing the previous example, I empathized with James by adding to the paraphrase and validation: "James, it sounds like you took a courageous step to confront your colleague. I wonder if that felt a little scary, too?" Here, I want to get at some of the feelings that are beneath the surface of what James shared. I mention both the positive—that it took "courage"—and what might have been difficult for him to do—feel the "fear." My hope is that by empathizing, James will feel understood and safe, and thus be more willing to go deeper and explore what motivates him to do what he does.

Since empathy involves accurately reflecting the feelings of group members, it is important for you as the group leader to be able to understand and communicate about feelings. The ability of group members to share feelings is important to facilitate healing and growth in your small group. If you are leading a small group, reflect for a moment on the content of what is being discussed in your small group. Is most of what is being shared by group members what they are *thinking* or what they are *feeling*? Are group members in touch with their emotions? Are they really sharing from their hearts?

As a leader, you need to develop your empathy skills. A key first step is your ability to feel your own feelings. How are you at identifying and communicating your feelings? Which feelings are most difficult for you to own and express? For most of us, the more difficult feelings are sadness, anger, and fear. The feelings that are most difficult for you to own and express in your own life will likely be the feelings that are most difficult for you to empathize with in your group.

As a short exercise, pause and get in touch with what you are feeling right now. Take a few deep diaphragm breaths. Slow down and deepen your breathing. Be aware of your body and how your feelings are connected with your body.

Are you feeling sad? You might feel tightness behind your eyes or a heaviness in your chest. You might notice tears. Sadness involves a broken heart connected to some kind of loss. Let yourself feel sad and be aware of the longing that is beneath the sadness and the need for comfort.

Are you feeling angry? Your neck, shoulders, and arms might be tight, and your fists clenched. There might be tears here as well. Be aware of how angry tears are different than sad tears; angry tears are hot. There might be a knot in your stomach. Anger is often about protection. What are you protecting with your anger? What is the vulnerability underneath your anger?

Are you feeling scared? Your body and heart might feel tight. Your breathing might be shallow or rapid. You might have butterflies in your stomach. What is your fear telling you? If you go underneath the fear, you might discover a longing for intimacy or identity. You might be scared that you are not lovable or valuable.

How about the more positive feelings in SASHET? Are you feeling happy about something? There might be a lightness to your body and in your heart. Your needs for intimacy and identity are being met. Are you feeling excited? Your heart is jumpy. You are anticipating your needs getting met. Something good is about to happen. Are you feeling tender? Your heart is soft. Your most important need is being met: your need for connection and intimacy. We all long for connection. It is what we were created for.

Work on letting yourself feel. I encourage group members to practice this daily. Three times a day, stop and ask yourself, *How am I feeling?* Then ask, *What is the need underneath my feeling?* Improving your ability to identify and communicate your feelings will help you communicate empathy for your group members. Be aware of the feelings that are most difficult for you to connect with. If we don't feel sad, angry, or scared, we won't truly feel happy, excited, or tender either.

Historically, I have had a difficult time with all those feelings, especially anger, sadness, and fear. When I was growing up, anger was not allowed in my household and was considered a sin. Sadness and fear were associated with weakness, so it wasn't okay for me to experience those feelings either. Boys weren't supposed to cry. When I was sent away to boarding school at a young age, I was told I needed to be brave. So growing up, I wasn't great at identifying and communicating my emotions.

This caused problems for me as a group leader. If group members expressed anger, sadness, or fear, I would try to smooth things over and move on with the content of the Bible study. As a result, group members stopped sharing their feelings. To help facilitate more vulnerable sharing, I needed to learn how to be comfortable with my own feelings so that I could be comfortable with feelings in my group. Your continued work in the area of feelings helps improve your ability to help your participants work with their feelings. Again, you are the most important tool you have to offer. Keep doing your work.

Clarification

As group members share, using the skills of paraphrasing, validating, and empathizing helps bring clarity to what is discussed. However, there still might be situations in which a group member shares something, and you don't understand what that person said. This can be a problem, because if you don't understand, the other group members are likely unclear as well. If the group isn't connecting with a group member who is sharing, this may lead to disengagement of the group and the group member feeling unsupported.

If you want more clarity from a group member, it's okay to ask for it. Invite group members to share more by asking clarifying questions. Be careful, however, when asking questions. Sometimes questions can actually shut down more sharing. For example, if you ask a closed-ended question (i.e., a question that can be answered with a "yes" or "no"), it is unlikely to spark deeper sharing. Group members may simply answer the closed-ended question and stop there. Also, questions can sometimes be leading or controlling, directing the participants to answer according to your agenda. For example, if I asked James a question like, "Why did you confront your colleague like that?" I am not likely to get more clarity. By asking "Why," I am indirectly communicating a judgment that something is wrong and bad about why James was confrontational, and I would likely get a defensive response.

If James does not feel judged by the why question, he will likely go into his head in order to answer the question and move away from getting in touch or staying with his emotions. James might say, "Hm, I'm not sure why. Let me think about that." Often group members don't know why they took a certain action or felt a certain way, and the why question can get them off track. So, avoid why questions. Instead, ask questions that will help group members share their story more clearly and more deeply, so that you can empathize.

Ask open-ended questions, which often are the best for increasing vulnerability and deepening intimacy. These questions dig for more than a simple "yes" or "no" response. For example, when James shared about telling his truth to his work colleague, I might ask, "James, you shared that you spoke truth to your colleague. How did you feel doing that?"

Before you ask a question, share the context around the question by first paraphrasing what you heard. For example, with James, I first paraphrased what he had shared (his confrontation with his colleague). My hope when asking this clarifying question is that it would lead to more and deeper sharing, perhaps even eliciting James's feelings around what happened.

Your goal as group leader is to facilitate your group members as they tell their stories. Facilitate by validating, empathizing, and clarifying. As group members share more clearly and get in touch with their feelings, it will be easier to validate and empathize. In turn, as you validate and empathize, group members want to share more and more deeply. In this way, you facilitate increased vulnerability.

As with the listening skills, you want to encourage your group members to also use these facilitating skills. Instead of you doing all the validating, empathizing, and clarifying as group leader, invite your group members to do so as well. Try to help your group members develop their abilities to validate one another, empathize with one another, and ask for clarification when they don't understand another group member's sharing. This not only helps keep the group safe and increase vulnerability, but it also helps group members practice these skills that are important for their relationships (both inside and outside of group).

LINKING SKILLS

Linking skills help connect group members with each other (Jacobs, Masson, & Harvill, 2002). Groups often get into the habit of individual members sharing with the group leader. Linking counteracts this habit and encourages group members to share with each other. Linking helps group members move from talking about content outside the group to the here and now of what is happening in the group. Linking helps bring group members into the group's interpersonal process. Because linking helps group members connect with and support each other, it is one of the most important skills to have as a group leader.

Besides the fear of rejection, one of the greatest fears people have about being vulnerable in a small group is being alone in one's pain. So many group members think, *No one is going through what I am going through. No one could possibly relate.* Because they fear being alone in their pain, they end up not sharing their pain and disengaging. Linking is the skill that helps group members feel connected with others in their pain. One great benefit of being in a small group is that others have had similar experiences. They may not have the exact same experience, but since your group members are all struggling, they have similar experiences and similar pain. It is disheartening to feel alone in one's pain, but it is freeing and hopeful to discover that one is not alone, that others can connect with our pain and suffering. When this connection and linking happens, participants begin to experience "carrying each other's burdens" (Galatians 5:2). There are two important linking skills to develop as a group leader: creating links and redirecting links.

Creating Links

Creating a link in your group is a simple and powerful intervention. After a group member shares, creating links involves asking the group, "Who else can relate?" For example, after Beth finished sharing about the loss of her marriage through her divorce, I asked the group, "Who can relate with Beth?" James raised his hand. He hadn't been through a divorce, but his dad passed away recently, so he could relate to Beth's feelings of loss. You can often see the relief on the face of the person who shared as they experience someone else relating. After one person has connected, I might ask, "Is there anyone else who can connect?" You will be amazed at how other group members are able to connect to the person brave enough to share, even around difficult issues. People really do have similar experiences. They just need a safe place to share their experiences and people who can relate. I am amazed how God puts people together in small groups who can connect. In your small group, no one needs to be alone. In fact, I believe that healing never happens alone. Linking is key to helping group members share vulnerably. As a group leader, create links early and often.

You can also create links before a person shares. Going back to the boundaries I set up in the previous chapter, in my groups, if someone wants to share, I encourage the person to begin by directing their sharing to an individual instead of the group as a whole. I call this "being in relationship as you share." This approach has three benefits. First, it facilitates relationship connection between group members. Individuals often pick someone that they feel can understand their story in a deep way. Second, it facilitates engagement and listening. Sometimes if a person shares to the group as a whole, it is easy for group members to disengage or stop listening. Third, sometimes you can learn more about group members based on who they pick to be in relationship with while they share.

For example, when James offered to share what he got out of Ephesians 4:15, instead of having him address the entire group, I asked, "Who would you like to be in relationship with as you share?" James picked Jane, and I asked James, "What is going on in you that you are choosing Jane?" People tend to pick others for a reason, even if they may not be aware of it. In our example, James wasn't sure what prompted him to pick Jane, but he said, "She seemed like she would understand where I was coming from." Asking group members to pick someone and share with that person what's going on in their choice helps create links to each other. In our example, James shared some level of trust and connection with Jane.

When I asked Jane how it felt to be picked, Jane said, "I feel tender that you trust me with your story." By creating these links while sharing, the group becomes more interpersonal in nature.

Redirect Links

In addition to creating links, a second important linking skill is to redirect links between the group members. Most group members, at least early on in the group process, direct their sharing toward the group as a whole or toward the group leader. This is natural and to be expected. Often, group members view the group leader as the expert and would like to hear the group leader's opinion about their story or a particular topic. However, the true power of a small group lies in having the group members help and support each other. The primary job of the group leader is not to be the expert who offers an opinion on each issue but to help facilitate interpersonal process and connection between group members. Thus, to facilitate linking and connections between group members, you need to redirect them to share with another group member.

Continuing the example from above, after James shared with Jane what he took away from the scripture passage, Jane responded that she appreciated James's insight into the passage. However, as she shared, Jane faced me and directed all her sharing to me, the group leader. I validated her sharing, but redirected her link. I said, "Thank you for sharing, Jane. I noticed that you're talking to me about James. I think this would be really helpful to share with James directly. Could you do that?"

Jane nodded, turned to James, and said, "Yes, James, I really appreciated your insight into that passage. I can relate to needing to speak up more to others." Now she was talking to James rather than about him.

Linking helps facilitate group process and promotes vulnerable sharing. As group members feel more connected to one another and less alone in their pain, they increasingly talk to each other instead of about each other, and if the group is safe, increased vulnerability and connection happen.

SELF-DISCLOSURE SKILLS

Sometimes group members may not know what it looks like to share vulnerably, especially in groups that have a lot of beginning group members. Or they might think they are sharing vulnerably, when in reality they are sharing about someone else, or just scratching the surface. In situations like these, it can be helpful for you as the group leader to engage in purposeful self-disclosure. Self-disclosure involves sharing your story as a leader. In the chapter on grace, we discussed how leaders have their own stories of brokenness, grace, and healing. These stories can be powerful examples for your group members.

Sometimes leaders shy away from self-disclosure. We might assume that because we are leaders, we need to be perfect or have it all together. We might think that if we are struggling, we shouldn't share our struggles with our group members, because perhaps they wouldn't respect us or want to come to the group anymore. In my experience, the opposite is true. Group members tend to be attracted to authenticity, which involves showing who you really are, the good and the bad. No one is perfect, so it is inauthentic to put forth a persona of perfection.

A saying I employ is, "Speed of the leader, speed of the group." In general, the group follows the leader's example. If the group leader stays on the surface, the group members stay on the surface also. But if the group leader models vulnerable self-disclosure, the group members share vulnerably as well.

Whatever type of group you are leading, my hope is that you will be doing your own work alongside your small group. If you are leading a Bible or book study, you are hopefully reading the assigned chapters and applying what you are reading to your life. If you are leading a marriage support group, you are hopefully working on your own marriage. If you are leading an addiction recovery group, you are hopefully working on recovery from whatever addictions you have. By working simultaneously along with your small group, each week you have something to share, and you can model vulnerability.

In the group I am using as an example, we were studying Ephesians 4:15: "Speaking the truth in love, we will grow to become in every respect the mature body of him who is the head, that is, Christ." If I am going to ask a process question to get the group to apply this verse to their lives, I should have already reflected on the question myself. How do I apply this verse to my life? What story do I have to offer? I may have a success story where I spoke the truth in love, or I may have a struggle story where I failed to do so. In either story, the content of the success or struggle is less important than the process I went through. What was difficult for me? What was my growth edge?

For example, I shared a successful story about speaking the truth in love to one of my colleagues at work. I shared how my colleague didn't hand in his work for the week, and that made it difficult for me to do my job. I felt angry and told him how I felt, and how I needed him to hand in his work on time. What was important and helpful for the group was to hear my struggle, my fear of stepping out and saying what I needed to say, because I didn't want to hurt my colleague or experience him being angry with me. The process was not easy for me, and the members could relate to my story. Because I shared vulnerably, they were able to share vulnerably as well.

Leader self-disclosure should be purposeful, done in the interest of the group (to model how to share vulnerably) rather than in your own self-interest (to do your own work). Self-disclosure should also be brief. It is easy when trying to model to spend too much time talking. For some leaders who talk too much anyway, brevity may be especially difficult. Work on sharing briefly in order to give ample opportunity for others to share. When preparing for leading your group, time yourself when sharing a story for modeling purposes. Try to keep your modeling under a minute or two.

Continuing the example above, when I shared my story, I did so briefly and did not put my self-disclosure out for the group in order to gain their understanding or support. I did not share for my own self-interests; rather, my hope was to model being truthful and real and vulnerable. I am very active during group and often share quite vulnerably. I think I probably share more than most group leaders, but I always try to be purposeful and brief.

VULNERABILITY EXERCISE: INDIVIDUAL

If you are currently leading a small group, reflect on how your small group is going. How interpersonal is it? What skills can you take from this chapter to encourage more vulnerable sharing and connection between your group members? Are your group members increasingly vulnerable in their sharing? If they are not sharing vulnerably, go over what we have discussed so far and ask yourself the following questions:

- How are you doing as a group leader in regard to having a heart of grace toward your members? Do your members seem to have hearts of grace toward one another?
- How safe is your group? Are your boundaries clear? Are you blocking boundary violations when they occur? For example, how are you dealing with the judgments that come up in your group?
- How are you doing at listening to group members when they share? Do you listen using the SOLER guidelines? How are you doing at paraphrasing and summarizing the content that is shared? Are you helping group members listen to one another?
- What about facilitating? Are you validating group members when they share? Are you empathizing with the feelings of group members? Are you helping group members to identify and communicate about their feelings? How are you doing at owning and talking about your own feelings? Do you ask clarifying open-ended questions when something isn't clear? Are you helping group members to validate and empathize with each other?
- How are you doing at linking? Are you creating connections and links between group members? Do you make space for members to relate to one another's stories?
- How are you doing with modeling vulnerability in your group? If you choose to self-disclose, are you purposeful and brief?

Reflect on your ability to be vulnerable. Are you able to model vulnerability in your group? Is being vulnerable difficult for you?

What experiences have you had with vulnerability that make it difficult? Identify and write about one experience you had when being vulnerable.

_____

_____

_____

Reflect on the vulnerability skills. Which of these skills are you good at? Which of these skills do you need to work on? Pick a skill and commit to practicing this skill. Write down your growth edge for vulnerability.

_____

_____

_____

VULNERABILITY EXERCISE: GROUP

If you are working through this book as part of training with other readers, complete these group exercises focused on listening, facilitating, and linking skills.

The first listening exercise involves _not_ listening. In your group, take turns being the sharer. Pick one person to share something from their own life. (Try to pick something moderately vulnerable.) As the person shares, the other members of the group will listen poorly. They will do the opposite of SOLER (e.g., be distracted, be busy doing something else, lean back in their chairs, look around). Stop after a few minutes. Have the person who shared talk about what it was like to not be listened to. Have the rest of the group share about how it felt to listen poorly. Once this process is complete, repeat the process with each person in the group sharing.

The second listening exercise involves listening well. In your group, two people take turns being the sharer and the listener. As the person shares, the listener listens well, using the SOLER guidelines. After the person finishes sharing, the listener tries to paraphrase what the person shared. Ask the sharer if the listener got it right. Allow the sharer to clarify anything that wasn't clear, and allow the listener to paraphrase again. Have the person who shared talk about what it was like to truly be listened to. Have the listener share what it was like to listen well. Once this process is complete, repeat the process until each person has the opportunity to be the sharer and listener.

The third exercise addresses validation and empathy. In your group, pick one person to be the leader and one person to be the sharer. After the person shares, the leader makes a validation statement and an empathy statement. That is, the leader validates the person for sharing (e.g., "I really appreciate you sharing") and also tries to understand the feeling that was shared (e.g., "When you talked about how you had to put down your family dog, you seemed to be really sad"). Allow the sharer to give feedback on the validation and empathy statements. Once this process is complete, repeat the process until each person has an opportunity to be the sharer and leader.

The fourth exercise involves creating and redirecting links. In your group, pick one person to be the leader and one person to be the sharer. At the beginning, the sharer starts talking directly to the leader. The leader redirects the link and asks the sharer to pick someone in the group to be in relationship with while sharing. The person listening then shares how they can relate to the person sharing. After the person relates, the leader tries to create a link, asking if anyone else in the group can relate to the person's story. After this happens, debrief. Allow the sharer to tell what it was like to have someone relate to the story. Allow the leader to share what it was like to create and redirect the link.

Truth

TRUTH IS THE FOURTH step of The Healing Cycle. For group members to heal and grow, they must face their struggles and growth edges with truth. According to psychiatrist M. Scott Peck (1978), best-selling author of *The Road Less Traveled*, mental health involves a commitment to reality at all costs. A person who is depressed must face the truth of that depression in order to heal. A person struggling with an addiction must face the truth of that addiction. Often we cope with our pain and struggles by hiding and blaming others. We all wear masks to hide the painful truth about ourselves, and in order to heal we need to face the truth about ourselves, even if it is difficult. Small groups offer an excellent context where truth can be given and received through the group members.

Truth involves giving accurate feedback about another person, when one person shares what is noticed or experienced with another person. To be helpful, feedback should be accurate and spoken in a context of grace and love. Giving another group member inaccurate feedback can cause harm if the person responds to faulty information, but giving accurate feedback can be challenging. Sometimes we may see the person clearly but fear that giving feedback may hurt our relationship with them, which might stop us from speaking our truth. Other times we do not see other people clearly, and our own problems and issues can color our perceptions. That's one of the reasons why it is important for each group member (as well as you as the leader) to be working on their own issues, so that we can see others more clearly.

There are many ways to test whether your reactions to another group member are accurate. It's a good idea to always assume that at least part of your reaction may be based on your experience in other relationships. For example, what about this situation reminds you of other experiences you've had? Another important strategy is to tentatively explore whether other people have similar reactions. We can usually place greater weight on reactions that other group members share and that occur repeatedly in a relationship over time.

In addition to being accurate, helpful feedback should be spoken in a context of grace and love. That is why I start The Healing Cycle with grace. Too often we begin with truth. Then we wonder why the truth didn't stick with us or the person we are challenging. In order to be received, truth needs to be built on a foundation of grace. The first two steps of The Healing Cycle, grace and safety, remain important as we venture into the later steps. Truth that is spoken with judgment or criticism isn't likely to stick. Even if the truth is completely accurate, it isn't likely to do any good unless it is given with grace and love. Giving feedback with grace and love says something about the nature of the relationship. People respond better to feedback when they trust that they are deeply loved and accepted for who they are. People have difficulty receiving feedback from people who tend to withdraw approval or use other manipulative tactics to control other people's behaviors. Grace and love provide the foundation for truth to be received in an open and nondefensive manner.

PSYCHOLOGY AND TRUTH

Truth is an important part of effective counseling. Many counselors believe that psychological problems are caused by problematic thinking (e.g., cognitive therapy; Beck, 1995). In other words, people are not in tune with reality or the truth about themselves and the world. These faulty beliefs and patterns of thinking lead to issues like depression, anxiety, or relationship problems (Beck, 1995). For example, depressed persons might have predominantly negative views about themselves (e.g., I'm a terrible person), the world (e.g., people don't like me), and the future (e.g., things are only going to get worse; Beck, 1976). Counseling might involve questioning or challenging the client's perceptions. For example, the counselor might ask the client to consider the evidence for or against a particular belief, or to think of exceptions to the belief (e.g., "So you have a belief that your coworkers don't like you. You have talked about your coworker Sally before. What about her? How do you think she feels about you?").

In group counseling, one of the primary ways that people experience healing and growth is through imparting information, which helps to educate and give people knowledge about their particular problem or issue (Yalom, 1970). Most psychological problems can be traced to interpersonal roots, but it is often difficult for people to see accurately how their own interpersonal behavior contributes to their reasons for seeking help

(Teyber, 1992). Except in very healthy, close relationships, it is difficult to get accurate feedback from others. One of the great benefits of group counseling is that group members can engage with each other *in the room*. People bring their full selves into their relationships with other group members—the good and the bad, the adaptive qualities and the rough edges. Instead of talking about situations that occur outside of the room, group members can experience each other in the here and now. Members receive feedback in the moment about how they are coming across to the group. The assumption is that clients are displaying their persistent interpersonal challenges within the group, which is a good thing, because then clients have a chance to explore more creative and effective ways of addressing those challenges. Group can catalyze people's awareness of how their way of relating to others is connected to some of the difficulties that led them to seek help.

This process of increasing awareness about the self through feedback is illustrated in a theoretical model called the Johari Window (Luft, 1969). The Johari Window is made up of four quadrants that represent different categories of information about the self. The first quadrant is the *public self*, which consists of information that is known to the self and others. Information in this quadrant is easily identifiable, such as a person's gender, age, and physical appearance. The feedback that is communicated about information in this quadrant is generally superficial. If group members' interaction stays at this level, little change or growth occurs.

The second quadrant is the *private self*, which consists of information that is known to the self but not known to others. Group members generally keep information in this quadrant hidden in their normal day-to-day interactions with others. Often this quadrant contains aspects of the self that group members struggle with or feel ashamed about. As discussed in the previous chapter on vulnerability, group members need to be able to share information about the private self vulnerably with the group in order to experience healing and growth.

The third quadrant is the *blind self*, which consists of information that is not known to the self but is seen and known by others. For example, a group member might think oneself funny, but in reality other group members experience the sarcasm as hurtful, sabotaging their relationships. Giving and receiving accurate feedback, the focus of the current chapter, is important to help individuals gain insight into truth that they may not realize about themselves.

Finally, the fourth quadrant is the *unconscious self*, which consists of information that is hidden from everyone, both from the self and others. There is potential, however, for the unconscious self to become known to both the self and the group as the group process progresses. Group members can then act on this new awareness to aid in their healing and growth.

CHRISTIANITY AND TRUTH

Truth is an important aspect of Christian spirituality, and it was an important aspect of what Jesus was about. When describing Jesus, the writer of the Gospel of John said that Jesus was "full of grace and truth" (John 1:14). To be more like Jesus, we need to have both grace and truth.

During his ministry, Jesus connected truth with growth, healing, and freedom. When speaking to his followers, Jesus remarked
that they would "know the truth, and the truth will set you free"
(John 8:32). Even though it can be painful to hear, something
about truth leads to healing and freedom. If you don't know or
understand the truth about your situation, it is impossible to
change, and you won't be able to make any progress toward your
goals. The same is true for your group members. They need to
hear the truth about themselves and their situations in order to
move forward toward healing and growth.

The apostle Paul also connected truth with healing and growth.
In his letter to the church in Ephesus, Paul encouraged his readers
to not be like infants or children (in regard to their faith), but
"instead, speaking the truth in love, we will grow to become in
every respect the mature body of him who is the head, that is,
Christ" (Ephesians 4:15). There was something important about
speaking the truth in love to each other that helped individuals in
the community grow and mature. If we don't learn how to speak
the truth in love, we actually cause our group members to miss
out on opportunities to grow into the people God created them
to be. Later in this letter, Paul gives another picture of how the
truth works to bring about healing and growth. Truth is about
confronting "darkness" and bringing it into the "light" (Ephesians 5:13). When issues come into the light, change can happen.

Another illustration I like to use when explaining the idea of
speaking the truth in love is the parable of the Sower and the
Seeds (Mark 4). In the parable, the "truth" Jesus referred to was
the good news about the kingdom of God, but I think the parable
can apply to any kind of truth that we want to apply to our lives.

In the parable, Jesus talks about a farmer who sows his seed on four different types of soil. We can think about the seed as the truth or feedback that is given, and about the soil as the context in which the truth or feedback is given. The first three steps of The Healing Cycle—grace, safety, and vulnerability—help create the good soil that is needed to nurture truth.

Jesus first talks about three different types of "bad" soil, in which the truth wasn't able to land and flourish. One type of bad soil is made up of the hard-packed ground of the path where birds come and eat up the truth that is sown. This might be like a group in which there is little grace present. Someone might offer a piece of helpful feedback, but because there isn't a context of grace within your group, it doesn't have the opportunity to land. A second type of bad soil is rocky soil. The plants spring up quickly, but the soil is shallow, so the plants are scorched and withered when the sun comes out. This might be like a group in which there is little safety or vulnerability. Group members may question the safety of the group or share at a superficial level. They might receive truth or feedback at first, but because they don't feel safe, they fail to implement it in their lives. A third type of bad soil is thorny soil. The thorns grow up with the plants and choke them. This might be like a group in which judgment or criticism is allowed to go unblocked. Truth might land, but because it is intertwined with judgments or criticism, it isn't able to grow to fruition. Finally, the fourth type of soil is the good soil. The truth lands, is received, and produces fruit. This might be a group in which the leader prioritizes grace and safety. Truth can be shared in a loving way, and it produces healing and growth in its group members.

STRUGGLING WITH TRUTH IN THE GROUP

Beth had really started to open up during the last few group meetings. On this day she shared more about her relationship struggles. Her relationship with her boyfriend has been very up and down. This last week, he told her they were over for good, leaving Beth distraught. I was proud of Beth for bringing this into group and vulnerably sharing her sadness.

Part of what makes a small group helpful is the opportunity to give and receive feedback. As I came to know Beth over the several prior weeks, my sense was that Beth had some issues that hurt her chances of having a successful relationship. For example, her mood shifted up and down. She was rarely calm or even; instead, she oscillated between feeling amazing and terrible. In relationships, Beth struck me as needy, wanting a lot of connection and closeness very quickly, but then pushing her partner away at the first sign of difficulty or struggle. This pattern had shown up in group as well; one week she got mad about something Edward said, shut down, and didn't return to group the following week. One advantage of groups—especially those that encourage members to share their interpersonal experience—is that members can experience the reactions of other group members in the moment, which can help them see how they tend to affect others in relationships. I wondered whether one of the group members would step in and share honestly about how Beth's behavior affected them.

When there was a break in Beth's sharing, Alice was the first one to offer Beth some feedback. Alice said, "You know, I was thinking as you shared. I realized I'm able to connect with you, because my boyfriend dropped me before Ted came along. I wonder what would happen if you prayed and asked God about this. If God wants this relationship for you, he will bring him back into your life; or if not, God will bring someone else better into your life, like God did for me."

Beth seemed to get frustrated when Alice said that. She was quiet for a time and then leaned forward and said, "I feel sad and frustrated when you say that, Alice. I'm trying to seek out God in my relationships, but it never really seems to work. Do you think that this is some sort of test God has for me? I hate that. If he's testing me, I guess I'm failing the test." As she said those words, she had tears in her eyes, but she also had a smile on her face and started to laugh.

Edward saw this as well. "Hey, I'm noticing that you are crying and smiling at the same time. What's that about?" Although I didn't think Edward's tone was the best, I thought it was good that he confronted Beth's incongruent emotions. But the feedback didn't seem to land with Beth.

After a few seconds, Ted jumped in and said, "Beth, just forget about him. There's a lot of fish in the sea. . . . You just need to keep on fishing." Beth didn't say anything in response to Ted, but it didn't seem like she appreciated his comment either. I started to think that perhaps this wasn't working. Letting group members speak their truth to Beth was becoming a bit of a mess. Beth was feeling hurt, getting more defensive, and starting to close down.

When I asked Beth if there was more she wanted to say, she said "No," and seemed to shrink back into her chair. The group moved on to another topic, but the discussion was pretty superficial. Beth was quiet for the rest of the session.

I felt frustrated. I sensed that Beth needed to hear some feedback on her relationship issues, but allowing group members to speak their truth got a bit chaotic. The truth seemed to hurt Beth, rather than leading to healing and growth. I wanted the group to be a place where group members could give and receive feedback, and "speak the truth in love" (Ephesians 4:15). I just didn't know how to make it happen.

Navigating how to give and receive feedback can be a difficult part of effectively leading a small group. Speaking the truth in love isn't easy. Think back on your own life. Do you remember a time in which a person spoke truth to you about something you were struggling with, but it was communicated in an unloving way? Write a few sentences about that experience:

_____

_____

_____

If you are anything like me, I imagine receiving this truth wasn't very helpful. Even if the truth was accurate, it was probably difficult to incorporate it into your life. Maybe the truth was said in a way that was difficult to hear. Maybe the speaker's motivation was in the wrong place, and the intention was to hurt you rather than help you. Either way, it probably wasn't very effective in helping you move toward healing and growth.

What about the opposite? Do you remember a time in your life in which a person spoke truth to you about something you were struggling with, but it was said in a loving way? Write a few sentences about that experience:

_____

_____

_____

This experience was probably a lot different. There were likely aspects of this situation—the speaker, the motivations, your relationship, and how the message was communicated—that made this a very different experience. It still may have been difficult to hear, but it likely had a different effect on you. Perhaps it led to an important change in your life. Our goal is to promote an environment in your small group where members are able to give and receive feedback to each other—to speak the truth about each other in a way that leads to healing and growth.

COMMUNICATING TRUTH

As you create a group that is characterized by grace and safety, and as group members begin to share vulnerably, there will be opportunities to give feedback to group members about their thoughts, feelings, and behaviors. Receiving feedback can be a very powerful learning experience, which is one of the great things about groups. Members can gain insight into their lives about things they may not even be aware of—that is, their blind self.

However, as we saw in the previous example, giving and receiving truth can be difficult. It's easy to share feedback in an unloving manner, and it comes across as judgment or criticism. In the next section, I discuss some skills that you as a leader can develop to give feedback in a helpful and loving manner. I begin by discussing general communication skills for giving feedback. Then, I cover using feedback as a linking tool, as well as some of the important differences between personal and behavioral feedback. Finally, I consider one of the most difficult aspects of giving feedback: offering negative or challenging feedback.

COMMUNICATION SKILLS

Some important communication skills can help you offer feedback to your group members in a loving way, which is also helpful in coaching your members to begin to apply these communication skills when offering feedback to each other. These communication skills include speaking for yourself and speaking in the here and now.

Speak for Yourself

The group members and you as the group leader need to speak for yourselves only. Speaking for yourself models good communication. We have access only to our own thoughts, feelings, and behaviors. When we speak for other people (whether in the group or in our lives), we tend to make assumptions. Making assumptions during difficult conversations can often lead to hurt, defensiveness, and escalation. It is more effective to speak for yourself, and let others speak for themselves.

The best way to coach how to speak for yourself is to use "I" statements. Using "I" statements makes communication clearer, because I am speaking for myself and not for others. When I use "I" statements, I take responsibility for my thoughts, feelings, and behaviors. Group members often say "you" when they really mean "I." For example, during a recent group meeting, Jane said, "You know how when you're a wife and mom, you kind of feel taken advantage of when your husband and kids are always asking you for things, but never ask how your day is." In this example, Jane is using "you" when she is really talking about herself. It would be clearer for Jane to say something like, "As a wife and mom, I feel taken advantage of when my husband and kids seem like they are always asking me for something, but they never check in with me about how I am doing." Notice how much clearer, more personal, and more powerful the second statement is. When I make "I" statements, I also feel a stronger connection to what I am saying.

Try it for yourself. Think about an issue you are having with a family member or colleague. Write a sentence or two about how you are feeling, but don't use "I" statements. Instead, write in the second- or third-person:

_____

_____

_____

How did it feel to use this type of language? Did you feel more or less connection to what you were saying? Generally, using second- or third-person language creates a distance from what you are saying. Other people sense that distance when they listen to you. Now, rewrite the above comments, this time using "I" statements:

How did it feel to use this type of language? Did you feel more or less connection to what you were saying? Did you feel more or less powerful? "I" statements are generally experienced as more powerful because they involve ownership.

As a group leader, get in the habit of always speaking for yourself, whether you are sharing your own thoughts, feelings, or behaviors, or giving feedback to another group member. Also, if you notice a group member saying "you" when really meaning "I," encourage the group member to speak for herself. For example, I responded to Jane by saying, "I noticed you said 'you' instead of 'I' when you were talking about how you felt. Can you say it again, and this time use 'I'?"

A similar problem happens when group members use "we" statements instead of "I" statements. "We" statements occur when group members speak for others or for the group as a whole. This is another example in which a group member is making an assumption that may or may not be true. As a rule of thumb, encourage group members to speak for themselves only.

For example, after Beth shared to the group that her boyfriend broke up with her, Jane said, "I think the group is [we are] being really uncaring." In this example, Jane is speaking for the group.

I said, "Jane, I noticed you said, 'The group is being really uncaring.' You are speaking for the group, but you can really only speak for yourself. Can you be more specific? What is that about for you?"

Jane replied, "Okay, no one is helping Beth with what she is dealing with." With her response, Jane is being clearer she is referring to the actual behavior of the group, but she still is speaking for the group by saying, "no one."

I prompted her again. "Jane, can you be even more specific? What is that about, for you?"

Jane then became more specific and replied, "Well, I guess I am scared that no one would respond to me if something bad happened to me." Here she spoke for herself, which led to a deeper level of sharing, as well as a deeper connection between her and Beth. Group members should continue to move toward speaking for themselves and not for others.

Speak in the Here and Now

In addition to speaking for myself, as a leader I want to focus most of my sharing and feedback in the here and now, and encourage group members to do the same. For example, Edward is working on his tendency to dominate and belittle others rather than love and humbly serve them. This pattern shows up outside of group, in his relationship with his wife, kids, and coworkers. Edward can benefit from discussing his experiences outside of group and receiving feedback. However, it is even more helpful to see the interpersonal dynamics of group members come up during group and address them in the here and now. This is where the power of group really shines, and as much as possible I want my group members to speak in the here and now.

I also try to encourage here-and-now feedback after a group member shares. Instead of offering advice about what a group member should do outside of the room, it is often more effective to encourage group members to share how they were personally affected by another person's story. For example, "What are you feeling toward Beth right now?" "Does anyone have any feedback about how Edward shared his story?" "Jane, it seemed like you had a reaction when Beth shared her story. What was that about for you?" Keeping a here-and-now focus emphasizes group members' affective experience of each other and what is happening within their relationships in the small group. It provides a powerful opportunity to learn new things about relationships, such as how to handle conflict, tolerate uncomfortable emotions, and take new risks related to disclosure or willingness to receive feedback. The more feedback and communication can stay in the here and now, the more helpful it is likely to be.

Using Feedback as Linking

In the chapter on vulnerability, I discussed the importance of linking, so no group member feels alone in their pain. Giving feedback is a type of linking. After a group member shares, other group members can offer feedback about what was shared, how it was shared, or how the sharing impacted them. People affect each other with what they say and how they say it. When group members share their stories, the leader and the other group members naturally have feelings and reactions toward the person sharing.

Feedback as linking happens when group members share how they are being impacted by an individual's self-disclosure.

Receiving Feedback

As we discussed in the last chapter, sharing vulnerably in a small group is difficult. Group members who do share vulnerably may wonder whether anyone else can relate, if what they said made sense, or how other group members perceived them. Being able to actually receive feedback about these questions is one of most powerful things about being in a small group. Often in everyday life, we might wonder how our behaviors affect other people, but we don't receive any feedback. Because of this, we are often left to mind-read and try to figure out how others perceive us. This process isn't very effective, and we often misinterpret how others view us. In a group, however, feedback can be received right then and there. The group member who shared can check out how the other group members reacted. Feedback as linking is important so that group members understand they are not alone in their experience.

Asking for Feedback

Although receiving feedback is an important part of the group process, it can be scary. Group members may not feel ready to receive feedback about their sharing, so ask them if they are open to receiving feedback before giving it. For example, after a group member has been vulnerable and shared part of his story, I might say to the member "Would you be open to some feedback from the group about what you shared?" Asking this question communicates respect to the person who shared. If the member isn't ready to receive feedback just yet, the member can say so. However, most group members are eager to receive feedback. After all, getting feedback is part of why they are in the group.

Personal and Behavioral Feedback

The two main types of feedback often shared in group are personal feedback and behavioral feedback. Personal feedback involves sharing feelings about how a group member's story impacted you, and behavioral feedback involves sharing reactions to a person's behavior in group, or the way in which a story was shared.

Personal feedback is often a safe form of feedback, especially for beginning groups. Sharing feelings in response to a person's sharing often is supportive and comforting to the person who shared. Sharing feelings can connect individuals in a deep way, so getting in the habit of having your group share feelings and emotions with each other is helpful in developing a close, cohesive group.

Sharing personal feedback also opens the door for other group members to do their work. For example, after Beth shared, I asked what others in the group were feeling as Beth spoke.

Alice said, "I felt sad when you shared. It triggered my own experience." If Beth was finished sharing, I might invite Alice to talk more about her own sadness and loss. Beth's self-disclosure triggered feelings in Alice that may reflect further work for her to do. By connecting with personal feedback, the door is open for Alice to do more of her own work.

Behavioral feedback is often helpful as well, because it allows group members to hear reactions to their actual behaviors and interpersonal interactions. However, behavioral feedback requires greater discipline from the group leader, because it is easy for group members to slip into a judgmental or critical tone. It may be safer to stick with personal feedback at the beginning of the group experience until the group has built up trust, commitment, and a sense of goodwill toward each other. When behavioral feedback does become critical, the group leader needs to remind group members of the boundaries of no judgments or criticisms in order to repair any damage and alter the course of the group process. Such minor adjustments are like driving a car; the group leader has to regularly make minor adjustments to account for conditions.

In addition to ensuring that behavioral feedback doesn't involve judgment or criticism, make sure that such feedback doesn't turn into advice-giving or caretaking. Listening to a group member share about deep pain and struggles can be uncomfortable. Many group members become anxious and feel a need to jump in and fix the group member who is hurting. Block advice-giving and allow for group members to share their pain. Such restraint on the part of group members can also be a great learning experience for those who feel the need to fix everyone. (The need to fix often involves a problem or underlying issue.)

Returning to the example from earlier in the chapter, after Beth finished sharing about her relationship struggles, I asked Beth if she would be open to receiving some feedback about what she shared.

"Sure, that's why I'm here," she answered.

I asked the group, "What were you feeling as Beth shared? Everyone just share one sentence and the feeling that you have. Stick with SASHET" (sad, angry, scared, happy, excited, tender).

Alice spoke up. "I felt sad when you shared. It triggered my own experience of loss and being rejected by a boyfriend in the past." Alice's personal feedback was very helpful to Beth, who no longer felt alone in her pain. By sharing her personal feedback, Alice connected with Beth about her story, even though their experiences were different. Although they had a similar breakup story, Beth's was shared through tears of anger for being rejected, whereas Alice's main feeling was sadness. But even these differences can be helpful, and they may lead Beth to further work. Sadness may reside beneath Beth's anger, and by hearing Alice share her sadness, Beth might be able to get in touch with her own sadness as well.

Alice's personal feedback also opened the door for Alice to do her work. If Beth was finished, Alice could talk more about her sadness and her loss. Beth's story triggered a story of one of Alice's breakups before her marriage. This might reflect unfinished business for Alice. By connecting with personal feedback, the door opened for Alice to do more of her own work.

Following Alice's feedback, I asked the group, "Who else has feedback for Beth? What feelings were brought up for you as Beth shared?" Two other group members connected with Beth's story and shared their feelings. This is a good example of using feedback as linking. After Beth shared her pain around her boyfriend leaving her, the group listened and empathized with her, and as a result she felt heard, understood, and not alone. The group helped to carry her burden (Galatians 6:2).

Using Feedback to Challenge

Receiving negative or challenging feedback can be one of the most helpful aspects of being in a small group. Your group members may be engaging in behaviors that are problematic and causing difficulties in their lives. Group members may not be aware of how they come across to others or how they are perceived. Withholding negative or challenging feedback may rob your group members of an important opportunity to grow and learn about themselves. Further, facilitating your group members in challenging each other is often an important skill to develop.

But offering negative or challenging feedback can be difficult and scary, both for you as the group leader and for your group members. That is why it is important to do a lot of work in your small group to set a foundation of grace and safety. (If you have not developed a foundation of grace and safety, you may want to focus on these aspects of group for a while before venturing into negative or challenging feedback.) As a small group begins to feel safe, increasingly invite not only positive feedback but also negative feedback or challenges. In order to heal and grow, we need to be aware of our blind spots. Giving challenging feedback provides that opportunity for learning. Confront them with the truth that you see. As you have continued to do the work of creating safety in your small group, and as you have continued to work on the plank in your own eye, you are increasingly able to point out the speck in your group members' eyes.

What kinds of things should you challenge in your group members? Sometimes this can be difficult to figure out. For example, what kinds of behaviors simply represent normal differences between people, and what kinds of behaviors represent problematic aspects of your group members' lives? I generally think about challenging two things in group: growth edges and discrepancies.

Challenging Growth Edges

As group members begin to share vulnerably and engage with one another, you can start identifying growth edges for each group member. I like the language of *growth edges* for a few reasons. First, it uses positive concepts of healing and growth rather than negative language of problem or dysfunction. Second, it normalizes the idea that we all have issues we are working on in our lives (i.e., we all have growth edges). Third, since we all have rough edges, group can be considered the sandpaper that helps smooth the rough spots that we all bring into the group experience.

Group members may have a sense of their own growth edges before joining the group. They may even come to group for that explicit purpose, such as when Beth shared that she struggled with intimate relationships and wanted to work on that area of her life. Also, as group members begin to share vulnerably about their lives and interact with the group, growth edges become apparent in your group members. You may notice growth edges that your group members aren't even aware of themselves.

For example, one group member might be too passive, whereas another is too aggressive. One group member might be relating to others intellectually but struggling to hear and respond to their emotions. Another group member might struggle to contain his emotions, letting them spill out all over the place, whether the context is appropriate or not. You might be concerned that some group members are struggling with an addiction to drugs, alcohol, or sex. A group member might be having an affair or is abusive. These issues need to be addressed for healing and growth to take place. Group members may or may not have insight or ownership of these issues, so invite group members into these difficult areas of their lives. Challenge your group members on their growth edges. Although many issues can be addressed in group, depending on your group context, some issues need a higher level of care than the small group can offer. If this occurs, you can recommend individual counseling so that the individual can seek that higher level of care.

Look at the various possibilities for growth and challenge in my small group. Edward is very critical of others, especially his wife, Jane. Jane comes across as passive in her relationship with Edward, as well as with others. She is uncomfortable with conflict and always tries to make peace. Alice comes across as controlling. She has a need to be right. She also seems to overspiritualize matters, especially if she is anxious. Ted is very talkative and tends to draw attention to himself and dominate the conversation. Beth wears her feelings on her sleeve. She knows what she is feeling and can talk about it, but she can also be volatile and explosive. She is often sensitive and easily hurt, and she is always late for group. James is really quiet. He usually never says anything in group unless specifically asked. He struggles to engage with others. When he does share, he stays in his head.

As you can see, lots of possibilities exist for challenging each person. One option would be to ignore these growth edges, but then you would be robbing your group members of a great opportunity to heal and grow.

What growth edges have you identified in the members of your small group? If you are leading a group right now, write down one growth edge you have observed in each member of your group:

_____

_____

_____

Challenging Discrepancies

In addition to identifying and challenging growth edges in your group members, also identify and challenge discrepancies. The first type of discrepancy I look for is in how a group member communicates. A communication discrepancy occurs when something is incongruent in how group members share their story. Communication discrepancies often happen when group members share uncomfortable feelings such as sadness, anger, or fear. When sharing stories that bring up these feelings, group members may try to hide their true selves, but the discrepancy reveals the conflict.

A good example of communication discrepancy occurred earlier in this chapter. Beth shared some of her anger and sadness with Alice but also had a smile on her face and began to laugh. Perhaps Beth was uncomfortable sharing her anger and sadness, so the incongruence was a way to protect herself from being so vulnerable. This incongruence may be outside Beth's awareness, and someone could challenge Beth on this discrepancy. This challenge would increase Beth's awareness of how she is coming across interpersonally and might also offer insight into Beth's discomfort with experiencing and sharing anger and sadness.

A second type of discrepancy is when group members' actions do not match their prior words, such as when a group member makes a commitment to do something but does not follow through on the commitment. There is usually an underlying reason for inconsistency between a group member's words and actions. If identified and challenged, this can be a great learning experience for your group members.

An example of challenging discrepancies between a group member's words and actions occurred with Ted around dominating the conversation in group and interrupting other group members. I had previously discussed the group boundary about not dominating the conversation, but with Ted, I had to be more specific, because he kept doing the same thing. Ted made an agreement with the group that after he shared, he would wait ten minutes before sharing again. However, in the next group after making the agreement, Ted jumped in right away, even though he had just shared. Challenging Ted on this discrepancy is important so that he can become more aware of the inconsistencies between his words and actions.

The wondrous thing about identifying and challenging discrepancies in a small group is that the discrepancies often happen right during group, in the here and now. Usually the other group members see and notice the discrepancy as well. As the group matures and develops, group members can help each other notice these discrepancies. The facts are there for everyone to observe.

Group members can work together to help each other live their lives with greater integrity.

Challenging without Judgment

Giving and receiving challenging feedback isn't easy. As group members begin to feel safe, they start to share more vulnerably, which can be scary for them. Group members identify and discuss core issues they may have been avoiding for years. Group members face old fears of abandonment, rejection, criticism, or abuse. In this process, they may once again feel the need to put up walls of protection and go back to old ways of coping. It may feel like group members are taking two steps forward and one step backward. This is a normal part of the group development process.

Although it may be frustrating to see group members share vulnerably and then retreat for a time, the walls that your group members use for protection need to be honored. These ways of coping have protected them for years and should not be torn down quickly. However, the walls do eventually need to come down in order for the group member to experience healing and growth. Your job as group leader is to challenge in love, which is often a scary process because you may be afraid of hurting the group member. Remember the ground rules for safety about no judgments or criticism. How do you as the group leader challenge without judging or criticizing?

First, you need to have set the foundation of grace and safety before giving the truth. If the foundations of grace and safety are not in place, the truth you offer to group members will not land. You will be wasting your seed of truth on shallow soil. Often in faith communities, people have the tendency to hammer each other with "truth," but they have not done the hard work of creating a context of grace and safety. Don't make this mistake.

Second, you as group leader need to have established a relationship of love with the group member being challenged. Group members need to know that you care about them and have grace for them *before* the challenging feedback is offered. Check in with yourself: How is your heart toward the group member whom you want to challenge? Do you feel grace toward this group member? Have you been doing your own personal work around how this group member triggers you? If you feel judgment instead of grace, it may be wise to hold back from offering your challenging feedback. It is also important to express grace toward the group member to establish a relationship of love. Have you been listening to this group member well? Have you been giving supportive and encouraging statements over the course of group? Have you been helping link the group member to others? All of these behaviors work together to establish a relationship of love and help build a strong foundation where challenging feedback can be effective.

Third, reestablish grace and safety after giving challenging feedback by following the challenge with statements that express love, grace, and support. I like to think of giving challenging feedback as a sandwich process. The first slice of bread is the context of grace and safety that you have created in your group, as well as the personal relationship you have with the group member. The meat of the sandwich is the challenging feedback itself. Then the second slice of bread is reestablishing grace and safety by expressing love and support to the group member.

Leaning into Fear

Giving challenging feedback to group members can be scary. Confrontation can be difficult, and most small group leaders do not like to challenge their group members. What about you? How do you feel about giving challenging feedback? What gets in the way for you? What is the fear about? Group members' anger? Group members not liking you? Are you afraid that if you challenge, your group members might not want to come back? What gets in the way of challenging your group members?

Most group leaders struggle to effectively balance grace and truth in their own lives and in the small groups they lead. Most of us naturally lean toward one side or the other. Group leaders who lean toward truth may struggle to create the necessary context of grace and safety. They might jump in and challenge too quickly, without first ensuring that grace and safety are in place. On the other hand, group leaders who naturally lean toward grace may struggle to step up and challenge group members when necessary. They might hold back, which robs group members of important information and opportunities for healing and growth.

If you naturally lean toward truth and tend to challenge too quickly or strongly, what is that about for you? What difficulties do you have in creating a group context that prioritizes grace and safety? What about you gets in the way? Are you committed to challenge in a loving way? If you continue to challenge without love, you run the risk of coming across as hurtful. Your group members may shut down and struggle to move forward. Commit to work on the plank in your own eye so that you can see clearly to remove the speck from your group members' eyes.

On the other hand, if as a leader you naturally lean toward grace, you may be fearful to jump in and confront your group members. Your group may feel warm and fuzzy, but people need to be challenged on their growth edges and discrepancies. Groups that avoid the truth part of The Healing Cycle tend to be more superficial, with members who never get to the core of the work they need to do. I am concerned when group leaders report that their groups never have conflict, which could mean that the members are not being tested or challenged. The apostle Paul wrote, "Glory in . . . our sufferings, because we know that suffering produces perseverance; perseverance, character; and character, hope" (Romans 5:3–4). We grow as a result of testing and challenge. M. Scott Peck (1987) wrote that to move from superficiality to intimacy, groups must enter into chaos. The challenge is for leaders to step bravely into the group's chaos and not run from it or smooth it over. As the group leader, are you stepping into the opportunities for testing and challenge in your small group?

Continuing this chapter's example, after the group shared their feelings toward Beth, I decided to offer some behavioral feedback about the fact that Beth said she was angry as she shared, but she was also smiling and laughing. I noticed this discrepancy (as did Edward) and was curious what it was about. Before I challenged, however, I started by affirming her: "Beth, I really appreciated you sharing so vulnerably just now. I know that took courage, and I felt really connected to you and tender as you shared."

After communicating grace and love to Beth, I brought up the challenging feedback. "Beth, I noticed something as you were sharing. You were saying that you are angry, and yet you were also crying and smiling. Can you say what your smiling was about?" While some group members may be unaware of the incongruence in how they share, others might have some self-knowledge in this area. Challenging discrepancies is an invitation to explore one's behavior in the here and now.

Beth nodded, recognized the discrepancy, and began to share how difficult it was for her to be angry. She was never allowed to be angry growing up, because it wasn't consistent with what a good girl was supposed to do. When she starts to feel angry, she often begins to cry, but she's not comfortable with crying either. She was not aware of the smiling and laughing as she shared, but after being confronted with this discrepancy, Beth shared her discomfort with anger and sadness—and how she generally runs away from those feelings rather than embracing them.

I followed up the challenge by reaffirming Beth and her work. I said, "Thanks for sharing about your history and connecting that with how you are dealing with emotions now. Emotions are one way we can really connect with each other on a deep heart level, and I want to encourage you to continue to practice engaging with your emotions here in this group—even the ones that are difficult and scary." Challenging Beth with her discrepancy gave her an opportunity to explore her incongruent behavior and see what lies underneath it.

TRUTH EXERCISE: INDIVIDUAL

If you are presently leading a small group, reflect on how the group is going. How are you at offering feedback to your group members? What skills can you take from this chapter to help you give feedback and offer truth in the context of love? How can you coach the members of your group to communicate truth in the context of love to each other? Consider the following questions for reflection:

- How are you doing in building a foundation of grace and safety in your group? Truth is most effective when grace and safety are already in place.
- When giving feedback, do you prioritize personal feedback or behavioral feedback? Personal feedback is generally safer, so if your group is still developing an environment of grace and safety, personal feedback might be better to emphasize.
- What kind of soil are you creating in your group? Are you cultivating the type of soil in which truth can take root for your group members?
- How are you doing with your communication? Are you speaking for yourself? Are you speaking in the here and now? Are you encouraging your group members to do the same?
- How are you doing in using feedback to link one person's sharing with the group? Are you being respectful of your group members in asking them if they would like to receive some feedback?

- How are you doing with challenging feedback? Are you able to identify your group members' growth edges? Are you able to identify discrepancies when they occur in group? Are you sandwiching challenging feedback with love and grace? As a group leader, do you gravitate toward too much grace or too much truth?

Reflect on your ability to give feedback to your group members. Are you able to communicate truth in a loving way? Which of these skills are you good at, and which need some work? Pick a skill and commit to practicing it. Write down your own growth edge for truth.

_____

_____

_____

Truth Exercise: Group

If you are working through this book as part of training with other readers, complete the following group exercises focused on communication, feedback, and challenge skills.

The first exercise involves practicing good communication skills. In your group, take turns being the sharer. Pick one person to share. First, have the person share something from the past. Second, the person should share something being experienced in the here and now. Get feedback from the group about the story with which they felt the most connection. Once this process is complete, repeat the process with each person in the group sharing.

The second exercise addresses asking the group for personal and behavioral feedback. In your group, pick one person to be the leader and one person to be the sharer. After the person shares something personal that is going on in his life, the leader asks the sharer is open to receiving some feedback. Assuming the sharer says yes, the leader invites personal feedback from the group (e.g., "What feelings did you have as the group member shared his story?"). Two or three group members should volunteer and share what they were feeling during the story using SASHET (sad, angry, scared, happy, excited, tender). Then the leader invites behavioral feedback from the group (e.g., "Do you have any feedback about how the group member shared his story?"). Two or three group members will volunteer and share behavioral feedback. Allow the sharer to respond to what it was like to receive personal and behavioral feedback. Once this process is complete, repeat the process until each person has an opportunity to be the sharer and leader.

The third exercise involves identifying growth edges in the self and others. Each group member identifies one growth edge as a group leader and gives some short context for or an example of this growth edge. Other participants are then given the opportunity to help the group member who shared identify other growth edges that may be outside of their awareness. Think of this as an opportunity to learn future areas for growth. When listening to others identify your growth edge, don't explain or defend yourself. Just say, "Thank you for your truth."

In the fourth exercise, participants identify and challenge a discrepancy. In your group, pick one person to be the leader and one person to be the sharer. The sharer shares something involving sadness, anger, or fear, but says it in a joking way or with a smile. The leader challenges the discrepancy in how the person shared and invites the person to relate the story again in a more congruent manner. Once this process is complete, repeat the process until each person has had the opportunity to be the sharer and leader.

Ownership

OWNERSHIP, THE FIFTH step of The Healing Cycle, involves taking responsibility for your part in a problem or conflict. When group members receive feedback about something in their lives, they can have a variety of responses. Sometimes group members deny that the feedback is accurate, and they get defensive. Other times they might think the feedback is true, but it feels like an attack, so they don't take ownership. Others don't take ownership because they think the feedback is more about the sharer's own experience and issues, which get in the way of giving accurate feedback.

Probably the most common reaction to feedback is deflecting the feedback they receive or blaming someone or something else for their behavior. Group members might admit the feedback is accurate but blame others for what happened. They might even blame God or a particular situation for why something occurred. If the situation had been different, their reaction or behavior might have been different. What happened was outside of their control.

The problem with denying or deflecting feedback is that it preempts any possibility of change. You can't change what you don't own. If the cause of the problem or issue is outside the self, the individual has limited power to make a change. However, if the cause of the problem is inside the self, the individual has more power to make a change. I often tell group members that it is actually good news if something is their fault, because then they can take responsibility. The real dilemma is if the cause of the problem is truly and entirely outside of your influence; then you are in real trouble. But upon closer inspection, we have some ability to influence all of our relationships through owning the ways that we think, feel, and act.

Ownership of an issue or problem is often a prerequisite for any real change, healing, or growth to occur. As long as group members deny or deflect the truth about themselves, they are just spinning their wheels. When group members blame other people or uncontrollable situations for their problems, they see little improvement. Blaming tends to get people stuck on what they wish someone else would do rather than attending to their own responses, which is especially the case when people are facing very difficult situations. Part of your job as group leader is to help group members take appropriate ownership of their issues, problems, and growth edges, so they can make meaningful progress toward their goals. As I like to say, "You can't change what you don't own."

PSYCHOLOGY AND OWNERSHIP

A principle from psychology called *locus of control* (Rotter, 1966) is related to the concept of taking ownership for one's problems. Some individuals tend to have an *internal* locus of control, which means they generally view themselves as responsible for what happens in their lives. If something good happens, they likely did something to bring about the positive event. On the other hand, if something bad happens, they are likely to blame themselves for the outcome.

Other individuals tend to have an *external* locus of control, which means they generally view other people or outside circumstances as responsible for what happens in their lives. Individuals with an external locus of control tend to blame others for the bad things that happen. They also place a lot of emphasis on fate or luck in determining the outcomes of their lives.

People who have an internal locus of control often function better in life than do people with an external locus of control (Cheng, Cheung, Chio, & Chan, 2013; Ng, Sorensen, & Eby, 2006). We can often take actions that either make things better or worse, so it is important to stay engaged in life. People with an internal locus of control feel as if they have more power to direct their lives in the direction they choose. If something bad happens, a person with an internal locus of control can take the reins and change course, but people with an external locus of control feel less power. They are at the mercy of other people or outside circumstances. Usually this perspective doesn't help as much for working toward healing and growth.

As humans, we generally have a bias to see ourselves in a positive light (Sedikides & Gregg, 2008). It's painful to view ourselves negatively, and we want to avoid feeling that way. In most cases, we are more likely to give ourselves the benefit of the doubt and come up with an explanation that paints us in a positive light. It's much easier to blame others or external circumstances for our struggles. This tendency is true in interpersonal conflict as well.

The *fundamental attribution error* says that we are more likely to explain our own actions by looking to external circumstances rather than our own personality or shortcomings (Jones & Nisbett, 1971). The opposite is true when we explain the actions of others; we are more likely to explain their actions by emphasizing personality factors rather than external circumstances. Thus, if we get into a fight with our spouse, we have a tendency to explain our actions by looking to external circumstances ("I had a tough day at work") and explain our partner's actions by blaming their personality ("He's such a jerk").

Taking responsibility for one's issues is an important aspect of effective counseling and psychotherapy, almost a prerequisite for any kind of meaningful change to occur. Sometimes counselors work with a client to confront the tendency to abdicate responsibility or blame others. At other times, counselors work with clients to help them see accurately what is within their domain to control. For example, you are responsible for your own thoughts, feelings, and behaviors, but problems arise if you try to take too much responsibility for the thoughts, feelings, and behaviors of others (Cloud & Townsend, 1992).

A balance is to be struck here. On the one hand, you want to support your group members and empathize with them. Challenging group members to take greater responsibility for what is happening in their lives can come across as judgmental. Some of your group members may have been in difficult or hurtful situations that likely contribute to their issues. But when people feel helpless or stuck, sometimes they stop fully owning their decisions in the here and now, which is like letting go of the steering wheel while driving. Things don't work well for long when people disengage psychologically. Group leaders face a difficult balance in empathizing with group members about the factors in their lives that really were outside their control, yet still challenging them to take responsibility for their current situation and make active steps toward recovery, healing, and growth.

CHRISTIANITY AND OWNERSHIP

Several examples in scripture show individuals taking ownership for their own issues and problems, thus leading to healing and growth. One such example is King David from the Old Testament. David had a close relationship with God and was a "man after [God's] own heart" (Acts 13:22). However, David also had a major moral failure when he committed adultery with Bathsheba and then conspired to have her husband killed in battle (2 Samuel 11). David then took Bathsheba as his wife, but scripture says that the Lord was displeased with him (2 Samuel 11:27).

The prophet Nathan rebuked David (2 Samuel 12). In the language we have been using, Nathan presented David with the truth about himself, of which David may or may not have been aware. But for David, his healing didn't happen until he acknowledged and took ownership of his brokenness. After Nathan confronted him, David admitted, "I have sinned against the Lord" (1 Samuel 12:13a). The ownership of his wrongdoing led to healing. Nathan responded and told David that the Lord had taken away his sin, and he was not going to die (1 Samuel 12:13b).

Psalm 32, written by David, offers a beautiful contrast between his life before and after he took ownership of his brokenness. Before he took ownership, David writes, "When I kept silent, my bones wasted away through my groaning all day long. For day and night your hand was heavy on me; my strength was sapped as in the heat of summer" (Psalm 32:3–4). But when David takes ownership of his brokenness, "Then I acknowledged my sin to you and did not cover up my iniquity. I said, 'I will confess my transgressions to the LORD.' And you forgave the guilt of my sin" (Psalm 32:5). In this situation, healing and growth came after David took ownership of his brokenness.

This theme of ownership is continued in the New Testament. In his letter to the church in Galatia, Paul encourages his readers to "carry each others' burdens, and in this way you will fulfill the law of Christ" (Galatians 6:2). This is consistent with the idea of engaging one another with love and grace. However, Paul also tells his readers to "test their own actions" and "carry their own load" (Galatians 6:4–5). In other words, we are called to actively support each other, but we are also called to take ownership and responsibility for our own issues, to "carry our own load." Part of leading your group well involves encouraging your group members to take ownership and responsibility for their own burdens and struggles.

STRUGGLING WITH OWNERSHIP IN THE GROUP

As the group developed, I felt more comfortable with truth and providing feedback to group members about the growth edges and discrepancies I noticed in their lives. I encouraged group members to give feedback to each other in a loving way. However, one difficulty I had was that group members sometimes struggled to take ownership of the truth about themselves. For example, Jane started group by sharing about a conflict she was having with her teenage son. He was usually a good kid, but he had seemed disengaged lately with his schoolwork and the family.

Jane's husband, Edward, responded and told her she was worrying too much, that it was just normal teenager stuff. Jane shook her head and seemed hurt by Edward's judgment. Edward tends to be really critical of others, which shows up in group as well as in his relationships with his wife, children, and coworkers. I got my courage up and said, "Edward, I have been challenging you about your tendency to be critical in the group. You have said that you don't know what that is about for you. I am wondering if you would be willing to explore that issue in more depth."

But it was tough for Edward to take ownership of the feedback I gave him. He shook his head and said, "No, I don't think I am too critical. Jane has a tendency to get worked up over things that are pretty minor. There's going to be ups and downs in raising our son. If she can't handle that, she's never going to be happy." In this example, Edward struggled to take ownership of his truth. Instead, he deflected and blamed Jane. He viewed it as her problem rather than his, which Edward has a tendency to do in group. He gets defensive and deflects anytime someone is hurt or bothered by something he says or does.

Most of us have a hard time taking ownership of an issue or problem in our lives, and this will definitely be true for group members. Even though they are ostensibly attending group in order to heal, grow, and work on themselves, owning their part of the problem is still hard. It's so much easier to blame others or a difficult situation.

Think about your own life. Pick one issue or growth edge that you have. Now brainstorm all the people (besides yourself) or outside situations that you could blame for your problem:

_____

_____

_____

See how easy it is to blame others? Owning our issues is not so easy.

Going back to our group example, Edward's comment led to some conflict in the group. Jane looked angry but didn't say anything and sat back into her chair. Alice, however, also got angry and jumped to Jane's defense. "Edward, you can't just blame Jane for your son's problem. Raising kids is a tough job, and it needs to be 50-50. Jane needs your support, not your put-downs."

That comment got Edward going. "Alice, you don't know what you're talking about. I'm not going to coddle our son until he's forty. I know what's best for my kid. Just let it go."

Whew, conflict can be scary! I probably should have jumped in there, but I wasn't sure how best to navigate it. When conflict erupts in group, it is almost always a sign that one or several group members are failing to own their part of an issue. In this exchange, Alice blamed Edward, and Edward blamed Alice. Neither person was able to take ownership, so the conflict escalated.

Even though this conflict wasn't resolved, I had the sense that if I had navigated the conflict better, it could have been beneficial for both Edward and Alice. The goal for this chapter is to equip you as the group leader to help your group members take ownership of their truth—to own their part of their problems, growth edges, and conflicts.

OWNERSHIP SKILLS

As you develop the foundation of grace and safety in your small group, members begin to share vulnerably and become open to feedback about their lives and growth edges, both from you as the leader and from each other. However, as we just saw, feedback alone doesn't automatically lead to healing and growth. Group members must be able to receive that feedback and take ownership and responsibility for their struggles in order to move toward healing and growth. Sometimes this process can be difficult. It's much easier to blame others or outside circumstances for our problems.

Earlier in the chapter, I asked you to think of an issue or growth edge that you have right now and to consider all the outside factors you could blame for your struggle. Recall how easy it is to blame others yet how difficult it is to own our part in a struggle or conflict. Now try to look at the issue in a different way. What is it happening inside *you* (your thoughts, feelings, motivations, or behaviors) that is causing or contributing to this issue or growth edge in your life? What part of the problem can you take ownership and responsibility for? If your first instinct is to focus on another person's behavior, consider instead what happened inside you before, during, and after the other person's problematic behavior, and how that may have influenced the situation.

After feeling so alone at my son's birth, I began to think about taking ownership for my tendency to isolate when faced with difficulties or struggles. But it still took a while for me to act. One of my colleagues at work seemed like a safe person, and I had begun to share vulnerably about some of my difficulties and struggles. My colleague shared some truth with me in a loving way. The truth was that I could not heal and grow alone. I needed others in my life. God did not create me to be a lone wolf in this world. He created me to be in relationship—involved and engaged in community.

At first, I didn't really think that the problem was too big. I was able to get it that my tendency was to do life alone, but I was so used to approaching life that way. My missionary parents sent me away to boarding school when I was in first grade. I grew up alone and had to rely on myself to survive. I didn't want to rely on others, because I felt like they would let me down. I had been hurt in relationships. I had evidence from my past, and I didn't really want to change. Little by little, however, my colleague and others continued to challenge me with the truth that I couldn't do life alone. I needed others in my life. At some level, I began to understand. I realized that I wasn't going to be the husband, father, and friend that God created me to be unless I was willing to take the risk to invite others into my life.

Still, I resisted. Part of me thought it wasn't really my problem. It became easy for me to blame others. I blamed my parents for abandoning me, my guardians for being overly harsh, the church for being judgmental, God for telling my parents they should prioritize ministry over their family, and my wife for wanting too much of my energy and time. I had trouble taking ownership and responsibility.

My colleague continued to challenge me, but with grace and love. I was challenged to take a look at my part in my struggle, understanding and empathizing with my past, but also encouraging me not to stay stuck. My colleague helped me discover my own role in continuing the pattern I had set up when I was young, challenging me to consider that, even though I had to rely on myself in the past, the situation was different now. I had people around me who loved and cared for me, and I could take risks to let them into my life. I began to understand and own the truth that I could not heal and grow alone. I needed others in my life to help me grow to become the man God wanted me to be. Over time, I began to own that truth for myself, which led to healing, growth, and change. But the process wasn't easy or quick.

Encouraging your group members to own the truth about their pain, brokenness, and growth edges is not an easy or quick process either. But as a leader you can facilitate this process. Four ownership skills for group leaders that I discuss here are modeling ownership, encouraging ownership, working with stories, and working with conflict.

Modeling Ownership

In the early stages of your group, group members might have a hard time owning their part of their issues, growth edges, or conflicts. Group members might not even know what ownership looks like. In previous chapters I addressed the issue of self-disclosure and discussed how a leader's self-disclosure can help in modeling vulnerability. The same principle applies with ownership. As group leader, you can pave the way for group members by modeling ownership in your own life and within the group.

Basically, you need to practice what you preach and teach. Look for opportunities to take 100 percent responsibility for your actions and for your part in any issues that surface in your life. Also, if you experience conflict with one of the group members, make sure you take 100 percent responsibility for your part in the conflict. If during the previous week you had an argument with your spouse, you could model ownership by briefly sharing what happened and taking ownership for your part, your actions, your feelings, the stories that you made up, and your needs. The natural tendency is to blame or hide, but the challenge is to take ownership and responsibility. As you model ownership, your group members can follow your lead.

If you are doing a Bible or book study, or if you are covering a particular topic in a support group, make sure to do your work. Were you triggered in the particular study for the week, and for what elements of that can you own or take responsibility? Be ready to share and lead the way. Remember the guidelines for self-disclosure: modeling ownership is not an opportunity for you to be the center of attention or to do your own work. Modeling ownership provides an example to your group members of what taking responsibility looks like. Be brief and purposeful with your self-disclosure. Remember: "Speed of the leader, speed of the group."

In the small group I led, I tried to pave the way by modeling ownership. For example, when we addressed the importance of speaking the truth in love, I shared how I struggled to do this, especially at home with my wife. I could share lovingly with others, but sometimes I struggled with being critical of my wife. Then I shared a specific example of how that happened in the past week. I took ownership of my part in the conflict and took responsibility for my struggle to speak the truth in love. After sharing my example, I invited others to share areas of their lives where speaking the truth was difficult for them.

In my example, I led the way by sharing my story first. As leader, you don't need to be the first to share, but it can be helpful. Modeling ownership is more important at the beginning stages of the group process, because group members haven't yet learned the norms for taking responsibility for their thoughts, feelings, and behaviors. The earlier you are in the group process, the more important it might be for you to lead the way and model ownership. As the group progresses, keep your example in your back pocket. Have it ready to share if necessary, but let others lead the way.

Encouraging Ownership

If you have worked hard to build a foundation of grace and safety, group members may naturally begin to own the truth that they learn about themselves. As group members see you model ownership, they may follow and begin to take responsibility for their own behaviors. It's amazing how this happens naturally when the first steps of The Healing Cycle are in place. For example, after I owned that I had been critical with my wife during the previous week, Ted jumped in and followed my lead. He shared how he, too, was critical this week with his wife, Alice. Instead of blaming her for their conflict—his usual behavior—Ted admitted that he was responsible for a conflict they had this week. He also went deeper and shared that the conflict they had was probably related to an affair he had two years earlier. He wanted us to know that they were in marital counseling and were working on restoring their relationship.

When group members step up and take ownership of their truth, validate them. In this way, you reinforce group members for taking responsibility for their own issues. For example, after Ted shared, I said, "Thanks, Ted. That took a lot of courage. I really appreciate you stepping up and taking ownership for your part in your conflict with Alice." I also shared some personal feedback: "I felt tender toward you when you shared that." You might also open it up for the group to validate Ted: "Can anyone else relate to Ted? Did anything come up for you as Ted shared his story?" When group members share vulnerably and take responsibility for their truth, other group members often respond with tenderness and empathy.

Sometimes group members need some encouragement in order to take ownership of their growth edges. Taking ownership and responsibility might not feel natural for your group members, even if you have taken the lead and modeled ownership. They might not know exactly what taking ownership looks or feels like.

If a group member shares a story but doesn't take ownership or responsibility for being part in the problem or conflict, a first step is to encourage the member to do so. For example, I could say something like, "James, I noticed when you shared about your conflict with your boss at work, most of your focus was on your boss, but I didn't hear much about your part in the conflict. What could you take ownership for about your part?"

At this point in your group, you can teach a bit about the importance of ownership. Sometimes I share about how we often have a tendency to blame others or outside circumstances for our problems, but this way of doing life leaves us with little or no power to change our situation. It may sound crazy, but it is actually a good thing if something *is* our fault. That way, we have the power to make a change. Of course, there is a need for balance here. Group members may struggle with perfectionism or overperforming within relationships, and in that case, they need to develop this insight and actually take on less ownership in order for their relationships to work well. Jane is a good example of tending to take on too much responsibility. For example, she takes in her husband's criticism and in the process loses herself and her own voice and power.

A second teaching point that often resonates with group members is that they can only work on themselves in the group. In other words, in the small group, we only have the power to change something about us—the way we think, feel, behave, and interact with the people in our life. If a group member spends a lot of time focusing on or blaming someone outside the room, a limited amount of change can take place, because the other person isn't here. (And even if the other person was here, the principle is equally true.) It's more helpful and effective to focus on ourselves and what we can change in us, which inevitably gives us some influence to initiate changes in a relationship. This is a specific example of a general truth that I try to get my group members to grasp: It's difficult, if not impossible, to change another person. The only thing in our power to change is our own thoughts, feelings, and reactions. The most powerful way to change the nature of a relationship with another person is to focus on ourselves and our own work.

Encourage your group members to think about and share what they can own or take responsibility for regarding their situation, problem, growth edges, or conflicts. If group members begin to blame others or outside circumstances, gently move them to focus on their own part in the struggle. What part can they own? What part can they take responsibility for? Over time, group members get in the habit of doing this naturally.

Working with Stories

Challenging and encouraging group members to take ownership for their part in a particular struggle, problem, or conflict is often enough to set them on the right track. They begin to take responsibility for their part, and this ownership sets the stage for healing and growth. But sometimes the situation is more complex. Group members may not be able to own certain aspects of their issues or struggles—at least not yet. Furthermore, group members may not be aware of their part in a problem, and it might take some work for them to figure out how to take ownership. If so, you can help work with the stories that group members present in order to help them unpack their belief systems and explore the stories that they make up about others and themselves.

Facts and Stories

The first step when working with stories is to help group members separate facts and stories. They need to be able to get in touch with and own their stories, and not make their stories into facts. Often when group members share something that happened in their life, or a reaction they had to someone, they share their story as if it is a fact. That is, they share their story as if it is the only correct interpretation of the events that took place. Group members need to understand the difference between the facts and the stories people make up about the facts. The facts are what would appear if a video camera had recorded what happened. We start with the facts, but then we add interpretations and judgments. Treating these interpretations and judgments as if they were facts is a problem.

For example, Alice shared a story about how her husband, Ted, got home two hours late from work and didn't call to let her know, and that he was being a jerk who was probably having an affair again. The facts are what a video camera would capture. The facts were that Ted told Alice in the morning that he would be home at 6 o'clock. Ted arrived at 7:45. Alice did not receive a phone call from Ted. The rest of Alice's sharing is her own story, which includes interpretations and judgments about Ted. The story might be based on past experiences, but it is still Alice's story, which may or may not be accurate.

Help group members separate the facts from their stories. Group members need to get in touch with the stories they make up, and they need to take ownership of those stories. These stories shade our understanding of what is happening, as well as our feelings and reactions. When other people hear us choosing to trust a blaming story, that can erode trust in the group and set a tone that leads to impasse and decreased cooperation. Stories often involve blaming and judgments, and group members need to take responsibility for the judgments they make.

Projections

The second step when working with stories is to help group members work with their projections, or how their own issues influence their stories. Projection occurs when a group member creates a story or judgment about another group member and shares that judgment as if it is true. However, in the case of projection, the judgment shared is actually a judgment about the person sharing and not necessarily about the group member receiving the judgment (Freud, 1915/1961). Projections are unconscious in that the people judging are not aware that they are projecting their own story onto the other person. Often the stories and judgments that group members make are connected with their own past and are really stories they are making up about themselves. Group members are often most judgmental toward the issues they struggle with the most. A good rule of thumb is that if a group member (or you as the leader) has a big reaction to anything, the reaction likely indicates that whatever happened is tapping into a deeper issue for that person. Group members should take an honest look at their own lives and struggles, and the judgments they make. Group members need to name and own their stories. This is what

Jesus is talking about in Scripture when he invites us to "take the plank out of [our] own eye" (Matthew 7:5).

Remember from the chapter on safety that one of the most important boundaries was no judgments. This boundary is very important for keeping the group safe, especially in its early stages. In these early stages, I usually block boundary violations and reinforce the boundary by reminding group members of the rule. As the group becomes increasingly safe, I still jump in and call attention to the judgment. Then I go further and invite the group member who made the judgment to do some work around their judgments, projections, and stories.

This work involves inviting group members to consider their story or judgment. When a lot of energy accompanies the judgment, it is most likely related to something about the person who made the judgment. Perhaps that person struggles with the same issue and is actually very self-judgmental about it already. Maybe what was shared in group is tapping into something about the group member's past or history that is painful and needs to be worked through. Whatever it is, the group member who made the judgment benefits from considering and owning the projection.

For example, when James shared about his struggles with being unemployed and having difficulty finding a job, Alice jumped in with a judgment. "I think you just aren't trying hard enough. When trying to find a job, you have to keep at it and be persistent. It isn't going to work to just send in your resume here and there."

I interrupted and invited Alice to do some work on her judgment. "Alice, when you told James that he wasn't trying hard enough, that was a judgment. It seemed like you had a lot of energy around that judgment. Would you be willing to do some work around that?"

Alice nodded. I think she might have surprised herself at the intensity of her judgment. I did a short teaching on projections, noting that when we have a judgment about someone, it may or may not be true about that person, but something about the judgment is certainly true of us.

I then asked Alice about projection: "Alice, is there anything about the judgment, 'You're not trying hard enough,' that relates to something you're struggling with right now, or maybe something from your past? Is there an area of your life that you aren't trying hard enough?"

Alice nodded, and she shared that she didn't think she was trying hard enough in her marriage. She also shared that her family was pretty critical of her growing up, and she heard quite a lot that she wasn't trying hard enough. By taking ownership of her not trying hard enough in her marriage, Alice opened a door to change and work harder on her marriage.

Laddering to Core Issues

The third step for working with stories is to use a skill called laddering (Neimeyer, 1992) to help group members go deeper and connect with the core issue of their story. Laddering helps group members figure out why their story or judgment carries so much energy. What about them or their history is getting so triggered in their story? Laddering helps group members take ownership for their part in a story or judgment by going deeper.

In practice, laddering involves redirecting group members' stories back to themselves and their own work. It involves refocusing group members on themselves and their own history, to try and figure out the source of the energy. One simple way is to start with the group member's story, and ask, "How is that a problem for you?" The question can be repeated until you hit the group member's core issue.

Continuing the example above about Alice and Ted, I asked Alice, "How is Ted being late a problem for you?" In asking this question, I am trying to encourage Alice to shift the focus from Ted's behavior to explore her own reaction.

Alice responded by saying, "I'm afraid he is having an affair." Notice that just by asking the first laddering question, we are getting to a deep underlying issue that obviously influences their marital conflict. If Alice was willing to do some work around her pain about Ted's previous affair, the laddering exercise could continue.

I asked Alice, "How is that a problem for you, if Ted was having an affair?" The answer might seem obvious—a partner having an affair would be troubling to almost anyone. But with this question I'm trying to encourage Alice to get in touch with her own feelings and reactions, rather than just focusing on Ted's behavior.

Alice answered, "If Ted were having another affair, it would mean that he doesn't really love me." Notice how the laddering question led Alice to go even deeper with her concerns about him having an affair. His actions (being late, having an affair) are telling her the story that he doesn't love her. Notice, however, that the issue is still focused on Ted and his behaviors. If Alice was willing, I could ladder again to try to see if I could redirect her even more toward herself and her own work.

I wanted to make sure I validated her work so far, but I also tried to ladder again, saying, "I get how painful that would be if Ted were having an affair and how that would certainly seem unloving. If you're willing, I want to ask you another question about how you are thinking and feeling about this. How is him not loving you a problem for you? What message or story are you telling about yourself?" My hope was that Alice would reach a core issue that she needed to acknowledge and work through. It may be the story of Ted having previous affairs, or if she was married before, of her previous husband having an affair. There might be a story of not feeling loved that she experienced from childhood. I wasn't sure what the core issue was, but I invited Alice to explore it if she was willing.

Alice continued, "I'm afraid that I am not worthy to be loved." Here Alice hit the core issue underlying this entire exchange. As she shared, tears welled up in her eyes, which often happens when a person gets to their core issue. You often see a physical response that I call a *truth response*. The person's countenance changes; you may see tears of sadness as someone shares their truth, reflecting the pain and brokenness at their core.

Laddering takes some time, but it can be a very helpful skill for helping group members access their core wounds and the messages they carry from these wounds. In this example, Alice became aware of one of her core wounds, as well as the message of this wound that she carries into her marriage. By taking ownership of that core wound and its message, she could begin to do some healing work. After Alice shared, I linked with the group and she discovered that she was not alone in her pain. Others could relate to her and were willing to join her in her work.

Working with Conflict Skills

If your group is functioning well—group members are sharing vulnerably and providing each other with honest feedback and truth—conflict still happens. Perhaps it's between you and a group member or group members themselves. Conflict can be scary, and leaders often have a tendency to want to avoid it, or try to resolve it quickly without fully working through it. Conflict, however, can damage group cohesion if it isn't worked through properly. On the other hand, conflict that is worked through can lead to insight, healing, and growth, not only for the group members involved in the conflict, but also for those observing the conflict.

Working through conflict is a major challenge for you as the group leader and a tremendous gift for the group members. You help group members move from superficiality through chaos toward intimacy and healing. You also model a healthy process of working through conflict and anger. Few of us have experienced working through conflict and anger in a healthy way. Group can be a place where that happens. In this section, we discuss some important leader skills for working with conflict in your small group.

Stop the Conflict

The first step to working through a conflict is to stop it. One mistake that beginning group leaders often make is to let conflict go on too long, which can hurt the safety of the group, especially if it is early in the group and an environment of grace and safety has not yet been established. When escalating conflict is allowed to continue, too many judgments, criticisms, and attacks occur. The resulting hurt and pain can be difficult to resolve. So as soon as you notice an exchange between group members become heated, stop the conflict. Face your own fear of conflict and get involved. Enter into the chaos and take charge. Say, "Stop!" Wave your hands or stand up if you have to, but stop the conflict.

Let's look at a conflict that surfaced in my small group. When I opened up the group to see if anyone wanted to share, Ted initiated and started sharing a story. He had been dominating the conversation during group, and Beth had had enough. She shook her head and said, "I am tired of you talking all the time. You're so selfish. Everything always has to be about you." I had to call her name, say, "Stop," and wave my hands in order to halt her. As group leader, I needed to make sure I didn't let the conflict continue. Hurtful words had already been said that would need to be worked through. Group safety was damaged and needed to be repaired. But this conflict was a huge opportunity to enter into the mess of chaos with the hope of coming through to the other side, into deeper connection and intimacy.

Sometimes conflict can happen very quickly, and I don't step in quick enough to stop it. I may not catch the first judgment or criticism, and the recipient immediately attacks back or gets defensive. Even if I do catch it quickly, the judgment may have already touched a nerve for the receiver, and the receiver attacks back while I'm trying to stop the escalation.

In our example, you could imagine Ted snapping back at Beth with a defensive or attacking response like, "What do you mean I'm selfish? You're the one who is selfish." This would escalate the conflict, resulting in both group members feeling angry and hurt. The safety of the group would likely be damaged and need to be repaired. Other group members also might feel scared and think that the group is not safe. As the group leader, your response to this conflict, as well as your ability to work through this conflict, is important for the group's continued safety and growth. The longer you let the conflict go on, the more likely it will become destructive. So, the first step is to stop the conflict.

Work Through the Conflict
The first step when working through the conflict is to summarize what happened and reinforce the boundaries of the group. This step begins to rebuild safety in the group. Continuing the example from above, I summarized what happened and then reinforced the boundary of no judgments. "Okay, we have a conflict here. Beth, you jumped in and made a few judgments about Ted. You said you were tired of him talking all the time, you called him selfish, and said everything had to be about him. Those were judgments. Remember the boundaries that we set up in the beginning of group: no judgments or criticism."

The second step when working through conflict is to invite the group member who made the judgment to explore what the judgment was about. Even though we stopped the conflict, the judgment still happened. Remember that judgments are often projections. While Beth made a judgment about Ted, it may or may not be about Ted. But the energy behind the judgment indicates that something was going on for Beth. I wasn't sure yet what it was, but I wanted Beth to explore it. I asked, "Are you willing to do some work about what got triggered for you with Ted?"

Here I was looking for a willingness in the group member to explore what the judgment was about. I wanted to help Beth get in touch with what was underneath the energy in her judgment and for her to own her part in the conflict. I asked Beth, "What was your judgment about for you?"

The challenge for the group leader is to work with the group member who initiated the conflict to explore what triggered the anger that caused the judgment. To the extent the group member who made the judgment can examine and explore its source, the less likely that the recipient of the judgment is going to be defensive or attack in return. In this way, you keep the conflict from escalating.

The group leader also needs to spend some time and energy on the group member who received the judgment, in order to explore that person's feelings and stories about being judged. However, I generally start working through the conflict with the group member who made the judgment and then come back to the group member who received the judgment. Often, once the conflict is worked through with the group member who made the judgment, the group member who received the judgment is less reactive because of observing the person who did the judging own responsibility for the conflict.

At this point in the process, I often stop, because when the person who made the judgment owns it, the conflict usually comes to an end. The person who made the judgment recognizes that the judgment is about him- or herself and not the person judged. I then link with the group. Group members are able to relate to both the person who made the judgment and the one being judged. Both participants in the conflict feel connected, and the group moves on.

Sometimes, however, conflict can get messy, and it takes more work for the person who made the judgment to own what the judgment is about. If so, I can continue with the following conflict dialogue process. The conflict dialogue has six parts (Facts, Feelings, Stories, Back to Feelings, Needs/Wants, Actions). In general, the process is directed at the group member who made the judgment. In order for the group member who received the judgment to stay in the process, however, I ask that person to paraphrase what the person who made the judgment says as we go along.

Facts. The first part is to identify the facts—what would be reported if a video camera was running. Ideally both parties agree on the facts. Continuing our example from above, I asked, "Beth, what triggered the story for you that Ted was 'selfish'? What are the facts?"

Beth replied, "Well, Ted had shared three times already today in group. This time, Ted talked for ten minutes and other people didn't share." Notice how Beth was able to stick to the facts. Often group members have difficulty sticking to the facts without letting additional judgments enter. For example, Beth might have added, "And Ted didn't care what anyone else might feel." If this happened, I would need to stop her, point out the judgment, and invite her to stick with the facts.

Also, notice that as Beth talked she directed her responses to me, talking about Ted in the third person. When helping group members work through conflict, I want them to talk to each other. So, since Beth began to talk about Ted but not to him, I responded, "Can you say that to Ted?"

After Beth shared her facts, I had Ted paraphrase what he heard Beth say. Then I asked Ted if he agreed with the facts. When working through conflict, both parties need to agree on the facts. When there is no agreement, the conflict can easily get reignited, which is another reason to keep the facts free and clean of any story or judgment. If I had let Beth slip in the judgment, "And Ted didn't care what anyone else might feel," my guess is that Ted would have difficulty agreeing to this statement as fact. Instead, he might feel the need to defend himself, leading to another conflict. But if the facts are clean, both parties can agree. Had Ted already talked three times? Did Ted talk for ten minutes? Yes or no? It is easy to agree when the facts are straightforward and free from judgment. I can bring in other group members to help with the facts if needed.

Clarifying the facts also helps both members of the conflict settle themselves down. When conflict occurs, group members react, stress levels rise, and group members go into fight-or-flight mode (Cannon, 1932). When group members are emotionally charged up, they are unlikely able to work through the conflict. It is difficult to think clearly when you are angry or scared. Getting agreement on the facts helps group members take a few deep breaths and lower their stress levels, so that they can productively work through conflict.

Feelings. The second part is to identify feelings. Remember the SASHET emotions: sad, angry, scared, happy, excited, tender. Still focusing on the group member who made the judgment, I ask what that person felt during the conflict. For example, I said to Beth, "Okay, thanks for getting clear on the facts about what happened. Now I'd like us to move to feelings. Using the SASHET emotions, how were you feeling when Ted was talking?"

She replied, "I was angry." After Beth shared her feelings, I had Ted paraphrase what he heard Beth say. Owning her feelings helps Beth get to the heart of what is going on inside her, and it can also help Ted understand Beth's perspective in the conflict. In this step, I simply have Beth state her feelings in the moment, but I return to feelings later in the process.

Stories. The third part is to identify the stories and judgments, and also work with the projection to identify parts of the self that may be influencing the judgment. For example, I asked Beth, "What was the story that you were making up when that happened?" I like to use story language because it helps group members understand that the judgment is a story they make up, which may or may not be true.

Beth responded with her judgment; Ted was being "selfish and didn't care about the others in the group." This was the original judgment that caused the conflict. Again, I have Ted paraphrase what he heard Beth say.

Sometimes the group member who received the judgment has difficulty paraphrasing the judgment. Having the judgment stated again could stir up energy in Ted, causing him to get defensive. As the group leader, I might need to help Ted through this interaction. I might say something like, "I see that those words are difficult for you to hear. I am guessing that you might be feeling a little defensive. Again, I will make sure I get back to what you are feeling and thinking, but first I want you to paraphrase back what you are hearing. This is a story that Beth is making up about you. It may or may not be true."

Returning to Beth, I said, "This is the story you have about Ted: that he is selfish and uncaring. What is the story you are making up about yourself? What is that about for you?" Switching gears from judging the other person to focusing on the self may be difficult and take some work. But there is the plank in the judger's eye. I want Beth to explore her plank.

There might not be an immediate connection between the self and the judgment (e.g., Beth might not view herself as selfish or uncaring), so I may have to help her explore. For example, I might ask, "Where in your life are you selfish? Can you relate to being selfish?" If Beth isn't connecting with the "selfish" part of her judgment, I might try to help her connect with another part of the projection. I might ask, "What about the not-caring part, or the talking-too-long part? Where do you see yourself talking too long or not caring?"

As the group member explores the judgment and begins to address where the reaction is coming from, I often see the countenance soften of the group member who received the judgment. As the group member who made the judgment takes ownership, the group member who received the judgment may not need to protect, defend, or attack in return. In fact, the conflict often is resolved as the group member who made the judgment acknowledges and owns what is going on internally.

In my group, Beth acknowledged that sometimes she does talk too much and that she was angry, but she wasn't able to connect with the selfish or uncaring part of her judgment. Beth was open to doing some more work, though, so I tried to ladder to see if I could get at a deeper issue. I said, "Thank you for owning your anger. What is that about for you that you were so angry? What was underneath the anger for you?"

Beth thought about it for a while, and something came up for her. She remembered that her mother would scold her when she was little, saying that she was selfish and talked too much. Beth also shared that her mother would slap her across the face as she said this. Beth tried really hard in her life not to be selfish, and it was difficult for her to admit that sometimes she might be selfish or hurtful to others. Again, I had Ted paraphrase what he heard Beth say about her story. As Beth shared her family-of-origin story, she began to connect with other projections of selfish and not caring, a common result as projections are explored.

Back to Feelings. The fourth part is to go back to feelings. After the group member who made the judgment explores the story and projection, I generally check in again with how the group member is now feeling. Sometimes the feeling may have shifted as a result of doing the work. I asked Beth, "You did some great work exploring your story. How are you feeling now?"

Beth said softly, "I feel sad and tender toward myself. I haven't thought about that part of my relationship with my mom for a long time." The person who made the judgment often feels sad and tender toward themselves and their experience. Again, I had Ted paraphrase what he heard Beth say.

Needs/wants. The fifth part is to identify needs and wants, which are often closely connected to feelings. When a person is in touch with their feelings, they can usually sense on a deep level what is truly needed or wanted. Identifying and owning one's needs and wants can be a huge step in working toward healing and growth. For example, I said to Beth, "I want to invite you to stay with your feelings for the moment. Just feel those sad and tender feelings. What is underneath those feelings for you? What are you longing for? What do you need?"

Beth said, with tears in her eyes, "I think I just want to be heard. To know that I matter. I didn't really get that from my mom. Maybe that is why I talk so much."

I also ask if she wants anything from Ted. She said, "I guess I want you to hear me, and when you talk a lot, I feel like I'm not being heard. I guess I want you to talk less and give the rest of us an opportunity to talk also."

I jumped in here and asked Beth, "Can you say, 'Give me an opportunity to talk also'?" I want her to own this want for herself and not speak for the group as a whole. Sometimes group members have difficulty owning their wants, but group members need to take responsibility for them. Also, a group member can have a want and make a request, but the other group member may be unable or unwilling to meet that request. It is still important for the group member to ask. After Beth made her request of Ted, I asked Beth, "Beth, you are saying what you want from Ted. What about yourself? What do you want for yourself?"

She said, "I want to speak up and share when I need something. I also want to know that I'm worthy even if I'm not talking or the center of attention."

Actions. After the group member who made the judgment works through the facts, feelings, stories, and needs/wants, actions may need to take place. Group members may want to make a commitment or identify a new goal based on the work that was done. For example, Beth shared that she wanted to commit to do some work on her relationship with her mom next time during group. She also wanted to commit to share in group, but also check in with group members who were more quiet to make sure they had a chance to talk as well. I discuss more about changes in actions in the next chapter on repentance.

On the other hand, sometimes no actions are required. The conflict might dissipate once group members really hear and understand each other. Imagine being Ted and hearing Beth do her work and take ownership of her part in the conflict. As a result of Beth's working through the conflict, Ted's defensiveness went down, and his heart toward Beth softened.

Also, after hearing the group member who made the judgment work through the steps and take ownership, the group member who received the judgment may be more open to considering whether anything in the judgment fits for them. I usually check in with the group member who received the judgment and ask, so I spoke to Ted. "Okay, so we have seen here that Beth's judgment of you really was about her. But I'm wondering if this might be an opportunity for you to do some work as well. How are you feeling right now? What, if anything, about Beth's judgment rings true for you?" I leave it open. Ted might say, "Nothing," but often Beth's vulnerability will open the door for Ted to be vulnerable as well. Ted might own and take responsibility for something about the judgment; it might fit, or it might not. If something is there, the leader can work through the six-step conflict dialogue with the person who received the judgment as well.

Working through conflict is complex. Although conflict is scary, it offers potential for good work. In the example from my small group, Beth was angry and made a judgment about Ted. This conflict marked a potential rupture to the group's safety. It was important to stop the conflict quickly and work through the conflict with both Beth and Ted. A lot of good work resulted. Beth was able to get in touch with some of the deeper issues that led to her judgment and own her part of the conflict. Ted was able to listen to Beth and have compassion for her instead of anger. Beth and Ted grew closer as a result of working through the conflict, and the group's cohesion increased as the members observed a conflict being worked through and safety maintained. It was a learning experience for everyone.

As seen in these examples, the process of working toward ownership of one's stories and conflicts can sometimes be focused on just one or two group members. I always try to bring in the rest of the members to get their reactions, though, because I like to keep the rest of the group involved. One mantra I like is, "When one person works, everyone is working." I want to give the group members who are observing a chance to share their work as I help Ted and Beth work through their conflict. At any time during the process, I might invite feedback and linking from group members so that the process is not just happening between the two group members in conflict and myself. In this case, I asked group members to share, "What was getting triggered in you as Ted and

Beth did their work?" This can be a great opportunity for the rest of the group to be involved and do their work as well. Conflict triggers everyone, and group members likely would have some reactions that would be helpful to share.

OWNERSHIP EXERCISE: INDIVIDUAL

If you are currently leading a group, reflect on how the small group is going. How are you doing at inviting your group members to take ownership of the truth about themselves? Are you modeling ownership in your own life and in your interactions with your group members? Are you encouraging group members to take responsibility for their growth edges? How are you doing at working with your group members' stories? Are your group members separating the facts from their stories? How are you doing at helping group members examine their own judgments and projections? Are you helping group members touch their core issues through laddering?

_____

_____

_____

How do you feel about conflict in your group? What is your reaction when conflict happens in group? Do you ignore it? Let it explode? How are you at stopping conflict when it occurs? Are you able to work through the conflict dialogue with your group members?

_____

_____

_____

Reflect on your abilities to help your group members take ownership of their struggles and issues, as well as their role in conflicts that occur. Which of these skills are you good at? Which of these skills do you need to work on? Pick a skill and commit to practicing it. Write down your growth edge for ownership.

_____

_____

_____

Ownership Exercise: Group

If you are working through this book as part of training with other readers, complete these two group exercises focused on helping group members take ownership and responsibility for their growth edges and conflicts.

The first exercise involves laddering. In your group, pair up and pick one person to be the group leader and the other to be the group member. The group member shares an issue they are struggling with. The group leader practices laddering. Listen, empathize, and then ladder by asking, "How is this a problem for you," or "What is this about for you?" Continue to ladder until you get at a core issue for the group member. Once the process is complete, switch roles.

The second exercise involves working through conflict. In your group, pick one person to be the leader, and two people to be group members in conflict. Have one of the group members identify a type of person who makes them really angry. The other group member role-plays that type of person. The first group member reacts to the second group member with a judgment. The group leader stops the conflict, summarizes what happened, and reminds the group of the boundaries. Then the group leader asks the person who made the judgment to own that judgment; the group leader also helps the participant in owning the judgment. Then link with the rest of the group.

If there is a desire to go deeper in the process, lead the group member who made the judgment through the conflict dialogue (facts, feelings, stories, back to feelings, needs/wants, and actions). The group member who received the judgment paraphrases what was said at each step. Link with the group when finished. Repeat this process until each person has had a chance to be the group leader and the group member who gives a judgment.

CHAPTER 7

Repentance

R EPENTANCE, THE SIXTH STEP of The Healing Cycle, involves turning away from one's current behavior and toward something new. It involves confessing the truth and taking ownership and responsibility for new insight about oneself, and then doing something different based on that insight. If a group member owns not putting any effort into the marriage, the next step might be to move toward engaging with the spouse. If a group member owns being critical and judgmental toward another group member, the next step might be to apologize and ask for forgiveness. Repentance happens when ownership of truth is put into action.

Repentance can happen inside and outside the group. Inside the group, your group members inevitably have conflict with each other and hurt one another. Repentance involves your group members taking steps to resolve conflict, confess their sin to each other, apologize, forgive one another, and reconcile their relationships.

Outside the group, group members can commit to repentance as well. The group can help support group members and keep group members accountable for the changes they wish to make outside the group (Hook, Hook, & Hines, 2008). Sometimes enacting repentance inside the group for an issue that may be impossible to resolve outside the group can also be helpful. For example, Ted felt a great deal of shame about his difficult relationship with his dad, who had died some time ago. Ted was able to confess his part in hurting his relationship with his dad and receive forgiveness and grace from the group.

PSYCHOLOGY AND REPENTANCE

Psychologists don't use the word *repentance* much, but a big part of counseling involves helping clients make and sustain concrete behavioral changes in their lives. In fact, one of the most prominent movements in psychology involved the shift from psychodynamic theories, which focused on conscious and unconscious drives, to behavioral theories, which moved attention exclusively to behavior, leaving aside what happens in the mind and heart. The founder of this movement, B. F. Skinner (1953), focused his early research on a field of study known as *behaviorism*. Working primarily with animals, he found that he could create behavioral change by modifying how animals were reinforced and punished. For example, Skinner would link pressing a lever with receiving food or drink. Lab rats would learn to press the lever in order to receive the reward. The ideas of reinforcement and behavior change are still used in counseling today (Hayes, Masuda, Bissett, Luoma, & Guerrero, 2004). This approach to counseling involves a tight focus on behavior and situational factors that can make behavior more or less likely. One key way to change behavior is to change the environment, rewards, and punishments accompanying the behavior a person wants to change.

Of course, although behavioral principles are very powerful, seeking to change is not always as simple as setting a new goal. Sometimes we may not even really know if we want to change. James Prochaska and Carlo DiClemente (1986) came up with a sophisticated theory for describing the process that individuals work through to address ambivalence regarding changing their behaviors. The approach is often applied to strong habitual behavior such as substance use or sexual addiction, but it can be applied to any area in which one wants to change. The theory asserts that people go through various stages when they try to make a change, and different types of interventions are more or less helpful depending on what stage a client is in (Prochaska, Norcross, & DiClemente, 1994).

The first stage of change is *precontemplation*. In this stage, clients don't yet realize that they have a problem. Interventions at the precontemplation level involve raising awareness of the issue in the person's life. The second stage of change is *contemplation*. In this stage, clients realize they have a problem but are still considering the degree to which they want to make a change. Interventions at the contemplation level involve weighing the pros and cons for a particular course of action. The third stage of change is *preparation*. In this stage, clients plan to make a change soon and are getting ready. Interventions at the preparation level involve getting a plan of action together, recruiting a support group, and making a commitment to change. The fourth stage of change is *action*. In this stage, clients are actively making progress toward their change effort. Interventions at the action stage involve changing one's environment and creating a system of rewards to reinforce the desired behavior. The fifth stage of change is *maintenance*. In this stage, clients have changed behavior, and they are trying to maintain the changes. Interventions at the maintenance stage involve continuing the interventions employed at the action stage, as well as dealing with setbacks and disappointments.

Groups are an especially powerful place to work through ambivalence regarding change. As discussed earlier, Irvin Yalom (1970) identified eleven therapeutic factors that he thought helped clients heal and grow in groups. Several of these therapeutic factors help people move toward greater repentance, or putting the ownership of one's truth into action and doing something different. These therapeutic factors can help people move through the various stages of change—from clarifying ambivalence and considering different behaviors, to trying out new behaviors, and then forming new habits that lead to long-standing changes in one's life outside the group.

First, *imparting information* helps educate and empower group members with knowledge related to their particular problem or struggle. Second, *corrective recapitulation of the primary family group* allows group members to resolve childhood or family issues within the safe environment of the group. Third, *socializing techniques* help group members develop tolerance and empathy, and improve their interpersonal skills. Fourth, group members can follow the example of other group members through *imitative behavior*. Finally, *interpersonal learning* allows group members to develop supportive interpersonal relationships inside and outside the group.

CHRISTIANITY AND REPENTANCE

Repentance is a foundational concept in Christian spirituality. Often conviction of sin (i.e., ownership of one's truth) leads to repentance. Repentance involves a confession of wrongdoing and a commitment to make a change and do life differently. Confession can be made toward both God and each other. In scripture, confession is connected with forgiveness and healing. For example, the writer of 1 John states, "If we confess our sins, he is faithful and just and will forgive us our sins and purify us from all unrighteousness" (1 John 1:9). Confessing our sins to one another is also important. The writer of James connects confession with healing, instructing his readers to "confess your sins to each other and pray for each other so you will be healed" (James 5:16).

Scripture offers several examples of individuals struggling with repentance, as well as engaging with repentance and changing their lives. One poignant example of a person struggling with repentance is the story of the rich young ruler in Mark 10. This man engages with Jesus and asks what he must do to inherit eternal life. Jesus instructs him to keep the commandments, and the rich young man responds that he has done so his entire life. Jesus, however, intuits that the rich young man loves and trusts in his wealth, so he instructs him to engage in repentance by selling his possessions, giving his money to the poor, and following Jesus. This was too large a price for the rich young man, who left the interaction with sadness. He was confronted with truth and opportunity to turn his life around, but he decided to keep going in the same direction.

An example in which an individual engaged in repentance is the story of Zacchaeus the tax collector in Luke 19. This story is also a great example of grace and love happening first, then leading to ownership and repentance. As Jesus was traveling through Jericho, Zacchaeus climbs a tree to see him. When Jesus passes by, he tells Zacchaeus that he will stay with him that day. The people didn't like Zacchaeus very much because, as a tax collector, he cheated them out of their money. But Jesus offers Zacchaeus grace and engages with the bond of friendship, and this grace starts a process that ends in repentance. By the end of the day, Zacchaeus announces that he will give half of his possessions to the poor and pay back anyone he has cheated four times the amount. Zacchaeus experienced conviction, and instead of going in the same direction, he repented and took the experience as an opportunity to make a huge shift in his way of life.

The writers of the New Testament connected godly sorrow with repentance. For example, in his letter to the church at Corinth, Paul wrote, "Godly sorrow brings repentance that leads to salvation and leaves no regret. . . . See what this godly sorrow has produced in you: what earnestness, what eagerness to clear yourselves, what indignation, what alarm, what longing, what concern, what readiness to see justice done" (2 Corinthians 7:10–11). While sharing vulnerably and owning the truth about themselves can be difficult for group members, just like Paul wrote, this "godly sorrow" can lead to repentance, healing, and growth.

One of my favorite verses about repentance is in Romans 2. Paul starts the chapter by calling out his readers for judging each other, especially because the people who were doing the judging were doing the same things as the people they judged. I often use this passage when I talk about the boundary of no judgments, as well as the idea of projection and being triggered by the things we struggle with ourselves. But Paul follows the passage on judgment by shifting his focus to repentance: "Or do you show contempt for the riches of His kindness, forbearance, and patience, not realizing that God's kindness is intended to lead you to repentance?" (Romans 2:4). In this passage, God's kindness is connected to our repentance. Kindness here is similar to the idea of grace I have been talking about throughout this book. A heart of grace and an environment of safety create the opportunity for vulnerable sharing and ownership of one's truth, which gives people a chance to experience godly conviction and repentance that lead them to change their life's direction.

Struggling with Repentance in the Group

I felt like Edward had made a major breakthrough in group. For a while, Edward had been working on his tendency to be very critical with other people in his life. This critical spirit showed up in his marriage; with his wife, Jane; and in his relationship with their two teenage sons. The situation had become so bad that Jane finally told him they needed to do something, because she couldn't stay in a marriage like this. I didn't blame her. To me, the things Edward would say to her approached verbal abuse.

Edward's tendency to criticize others showed up in group as well. Edward struggled to maintain the boundaries regarding no judgments or criticisms. At first, he would deny he was even making a judgment. When confronted about it, he would say that he "was only trying to help." He would also use his religion to cover up his judgments, saying that he was "just trying to call out sin."

I gave him grace. I was careful to temper my own attitudes toward Edward, believing that he could grow and change. However, I was consistent in maintaining the boundaries, and I stopped him whenever he judged or criticized.

Beth had confronted Alice for spiritualizing things in group. Something triggered Edward, and he criticized Beth for being too judgmental. I was taken aback by how blatant the projection was—Edward, the judgmental group member, growing angry and confronting Beth for being judgmental. I jumped in and invited Edward to explore his judgment. Edward may have been surprised at how triggered he was, and he agreed to do some work around this issue. He saw the connection between his judgment and his tendency to criticize, and he did some work around his relationship with his dad, who was very critical with Edward during his growing-up years.

Something still seemed missing, however. Even though Edward was able to achieve some insight into his patterns of behavior, I wasn't sure if anything actually changed inside him. Was insight enough? Would understanding the connections between his critical dad and his own tendency to be critical be enough to change Edward's behavior? Would he become less critical with Jane and his sons? Would he become less critical in the group?

Some business between Edward and Beth also seemed unfinished. In the last chapter, we discussed the power of seeing a group member who made a critical remark make themselves vulnerable and work on their issue in front of the group. Often this step can soften the heart of the person who received the judgment, because the recipient understands that the judgment was mainly about the person who made it. I did see this happen some with Beth as Edward did his work. However, she still seemed hurt, which made me wonder if I could have done more to facilitate forgiveness and reconciliation between Edward and Beth.

During check-in the following week, Jane was upset. She checked in feeling sad and angry, particularly about her relationship with Edward. She shared that she left group the previous week feeling happy, excited, and hopeful, because of the work Edward had done in group. She thought they had turned a corner, and that things would be different moving forward. However, she reported that this week had been more of the same. Edward had been critical with her about several different issues, including her parenting and how she looked. One night the situation was so bad that Jane had to leave the house. She had been so hopeful last week, but now it seemed like life was never going to get any better.

As group leader, this was difficult for me to hear. Edward seemed like he had done so much work and made so much progress. But then came the disconnect in the following week between the insight he had received and his actual behavior. Edward had owned his truth, but the ownership hadn't led to a change.

This problem is common in small groups, and in life in general. It's difficult to actually change one's behavior, whether it is something simple, like biting your nails, or something more complex, like Edward's tendency to be too critical in his relationships.

Think about your own situation. Pick one growth edge that you are working on. How long have you been working on this growth edge and why?

_____

_____

_____

Write about a time where you tried to make a change on this issue and it didn't work out:

_____

_____

_____

The purpose of these questions is to help us remember how tough it is to actually change something. It's difficult for anyone to turn away from their old ways and start moving in a different direction, but that is our ultimate hope when we lead small groups. We hope that what our members experience in group will translate into actual changes in their lives, inside and outside the group. We hope that our group members will have a "new walk." The goal for this chapter is to assist you as the group leader in helping your group members translate the things they learn in group about themselves into actual behavior change.

Repentance Skills

As group members begin to own the truth that they are learning about themselves in group, they will want to do something about it. As the last step of The Healing Cycle, repentance involves taking the new learning that group members gain about themselves and putting it into practice inside and outside the group.

Think about one issue or growth edge in your own life that you have struggled with, but on which you have been able to make some progress over the years. When you finally took ownership of your problem, what did you do? What did it look like to put ownership of your truth into action?

_____

_____

_____

For me, once I acknowledged that I had a tendency to isolate and do life alone, I realized that I wanted to make some changes. I had to confess to God my tendency to isolate, but also to my wife, Cheryl. I had to apologize, ask for forgiveness, and take steps to repair that relationship. I also had to put consistent effort into reaching out to others with my pain and struggles, which felt unnatural at first because it was completely new to me. My messages from childhood would creep back up into my consciousness, telling me I couldn't trust anyone but myself. I had to fight these messages and continue to reach out for a different experience. I also committed to being in a small group with other men, making the effort to be open and honest with these men about what was happening with me. This small group experience allowed me to continue to work on my tendency to isolate, and the small group itself challenged this tendency, because I was meeting regularly with other men. Even though I have grown in this area, I'm not perfect. Especially when things get tough, I still want to isolate, and sometimes I still do. When this happens, I need to give myself grace and work through the steps of The Healing Cycle again. The journey of healing and growth is ongoing.

Group leaders sometimes struggle when group members seem to take ownership of a truth about themselves during group but then go home and continue to struggle with the exact same issue. Maybe they seem to make progress on a growth edge during group, but then the same matter arises during the very next session. (Think of Edward working hard on not being so critical toward Jane and their boys. He would do okay for a while but then revert to his old ways and hurting his family.) Group leaders can become disheartened when it seems like group members aren't making much progress at all.

Part of the work is realizing that change is a slow process. Sometimes it seems as if group members are taking two steps forward and one step backward, or perhaps even one step forward and two steps backward. This is real life, and quick fixes for deep struggles don't usually exist. Still, we can do some things as leaders to help group members put ownership of their truth into action. In the next sections, we discuss several repentance skills. These skills include things that you can do during the small group session to repair relationships after conflict in the group, help group members make changes outside the group, and assist group members in dealing with setbacks.

RELATIONSHIP REPAIR SKILLS

In the previous chapter, I talked about how to work through conflict with your group members. Although conflict can be scary, if worked through effectively, conflict can lead to significant changes in your group members. However, the group may also need to work through relationship pain after conflict occurs. As group leader, you want to be able to process and work through this relational pain in order to strengthen the relationships between group members as well as your group's general cohesion. Reinforcing these skills with your group members also helps them improve relationships with their friends, family members, and colleagues outside of group. Four types of relationship repair skills are important to develop: confession, apology, forgiveness, and reconciliation skills.

Confession

Confession involves admitting one's struggles and faults to God and each other. It is the practice of making ownership of one's truth public. One important benefit of being in a small group is the context it provides for individuals to confess their sin to one another. Group is often a great conduit for forgiveness and healing to take place.

I think it is important to confess our struggles and faults both to

God and to one another. Sometimes in my sex addiction groups, I ask group members if they have confessed their addiction to anyone. Group members who are religious often say that they have confessed their addiction to God; some have done so time and time again. I then ask if they have confessed their addiction to anyone else. Many have not. Their addiction is a secret between them and God, which may offer one reason why people in the church sometimes experience little healing.

Although confessing our sins to God is an important first step, it is usually (perhaps almost always) an important part of the process to confess our sins to other people, too. Something about confessing to another person leads to healing in a unique way by bringing into the open our ownership of the truth. A secret is like an infected wound. Confessing to others brings the wound into the light so that it can be cleaned and worked on openly.

In my small group, following the conflict between Edward and Beth, Edward did some work around his part in the conflict, including some of his early experiences with his dad. I could notice Beth's heart softening toward Edward as he did his work, but I sensed that she was still angry about what happened and that some unfinished business remained. After Edward had done his work, I asked whether he wanted to say or confess anything to Beth about what happened.

Edward slowly nodded and said he wanted to say he was sorry for getting so angry and lashing out. He was saying this to me as the group leader, so I encouraged him to say it to Beth. He turned toward Beth and said he wanted to confess his anger and lashing out, and that it wasn't right for him to treat her that way.

Apology

Confession often leads to an apology, which involves acknowledging to others responsibility and regret for how one's behavior affected another person. Apologies are powerful. One can never change the past, but apologies can change how we think about the past, and they can also give us more assurance that future offenses are less likely to occur again. A good apology communicates that one feels responsible, regrets the offense, and plans to take necessary steps to repair the damage and prevent similar offenses from occurring in the future. Because it generally comes out of a place of acknowledging responsibility (e.g., "I caused this hurt"), an apology is usually an important step for helping group members work toward forgiveness and reconciliation. In giving an apology, group members own their truth and make it public for the group to see.

Good apologies also take effort. Apologies that are too brief can come across as dismissive, or they might even indicate a lack of seriousness about the offense. Johanna Kirchhoff and colleagues (2009) have done research on how to give an effective apology, and they say that good apologies generally have ten parts; it's more than just saying, "I'm sorry," and moving on. The ten parts of a good apology help communicate to the victim that the person who instigated the hurt is sincerely sorry and wants to make amends.

1. *Give a statement of apology.* The first part is self-explanatory—you make a statement of the apology. An example of this would be saying, "I'm sorry," or "I apologize."

2. *Name the offense.* Say what the offense was. Some people have a tendency to say, "I'm sorry," but it isn't clear what the person is sorry for. It's better to be clear and name the offense.

3. *Take responsibility for the offense.* Acknowledge that you were the cause of the offense. This relates to the previous chapter on the importance of ownership. A good apology takes responsibility rather than blaming others.

4. *Explain the offense but don't explain away the offense.* It's usually a good idea to have some explanation for the offense, so the person who was hurt can understand what was happening. This can be an important element in increasing empathy in the person who was hurt. However, be careful that the explanation doesn't explain away the offense; responsibility is key.

5. *Convey emotions.* Express emotion when giving the apology. For example, if you are feeling sad, let the other person in on the sadness. This can increase empathy for the offending party.

6. *Address the emotions of and/or damage to the offended person.* Acknowledge and address the repercussions of the hurt. Our actions have consequences, and a proper apology lets the person know that you understand these consequences.

7. *Admit fault.* This point is similar to taking responsibility. It helps to say directly, "It was my fault."

8. *Promise forbearance.* One thing making forgiveness difficult for the hurt party is the fear of being hurt again. Describe the lessons that you learned and the changes

you will make to ensure that you will not hurt the person in the same way moving forward.

9. *Offer reparation.* Reparations aren't always applicable, but offering something can be helpful to make up for the hurt that was done. For example, if you borrowed a friend's shirt and stained it, you can offer to replace the shirt.

10. *Request apology acceptance.* Sometimes an apology is given and the person who was hurt doesn't respond. It can be helpful to ask the person who was hurt to accept the apology.

In the example from my group, Edward had already started to give an apology as part of his confession to Beth and the group about his anger and lashing out. His apology was a good start—he gave a statement of the apology ("I'm sorry"), and he named the offense ("I got angry and lashed out"). I thought he could do more here, so I encouraged him to go deeper with his apology. I said, "Edward, thank you for apologizing to Beth. I think that's a big step for you, and it's really important to help mend your relationship with Beth, as well as with the rest of the group. I'm wondering if you could say a bit more about what was going on with you when you lashed out, and how you are feeling now."

Edward nodded, and he talked about how he realized now that he was triggered when Beth confronted Alice, and the anger was coming out of his own issues with his dad. His dad had been critical of him growing up. It was a huge wound, and Edward had learned to cope with it by doing just what his dad modeled: being critical. Edward also shared that he was feeling sad that he had hurt Beth, and he hoped that he could do a better job of supporting Beth moving forward. Beth seemed genuinely moved by Edward's apology. She said she appreciated Edward's words, and she accepted his apology. What seemed different about Edward this time was the congruence of his emotions and behavior with his comments. He seemed to really get it. He actually had tears in his eyes.

Forgiveness

Forgiveness involves changes that occur inside the victim toward the person who delivered the hurt. These changes can involve fewer negative and more positive thoughts, feelings, motivations, and actual behaviors. Facilitating forgiveness between two group members who have hurt each other can be a powerful intervention that can assist with reconciliation and restore group cohesion following a conflict or hurt.

Psychologist Everett Worthington (1998) has developed an intervention to help people work through forgiveness. The process, which you can lead members through, is represented by the acronym REACH—for recall, empathy, altruism, commitment, and holding on.

The first step is to *recall the hurt in a neutral way*. People who are struggling with forgiveness often think about what happened in an angry, spiteful way. They might ruminate about the offense and think about what they would do to take revenge on the person who hurt them. Recalling the hurt in a neutral way can help counteract this tendency. You could ask group members to think about the hurt as if a news reporter or video camera was replaying what happened.

The second step is to *empathize with the person who hurt you*. Empathy involves taking the perspective of the other person and actually feeling what it would be like to be that person. Empathy is one of the strongest and most consistent predictors of forgiveness (McCullough, Worthington, & Rachal, 1997). One exercise to help group members experience empathy for the person who hurt them is to lead them through the 5 *p*'s. In this exercise, group members think about various factors that may have led to the person committing the offense, including (1) external *pressures*, (2) *past* hurts of their own, (3) *personality* traits (e.g., high anxiety), (4) feeling *provoked*, or (5) good intentions (i.e., an original *plan*) gone awry.

The third step is to give an *altruistic gift of forgiveness*. Some individuals, especially those who are religious, may feel pressure to forgive, because they were taught that forgiveness is required to be a good Christian. This pressure can actually get in the way of a person who is trying to forgive. In contrast, I like to think about forgiveness as an altruistic gift that a person can choose to give or not give. Some exercises that can help promote a sense of altruism include having the person think about a time when an offense was committed, which leads to *humility*, and having the person think about a time when forgiveness was received, which leads to *gratitude*.

The fourth step is to *commit to forgiveness*. Sometimes it is helpful to take a concrete or physical action to indicate this commitment. These sorts of exercises can be incredibly powerful when conducted in a group setting. For example, one group member could create a certificate of forgiveness and present it to the offending group member. Similarly, one group member could write a letter of forgiveness and read it out loud to another group member. A third exercise is to have a group member write a description of the hurt on his hand with a marker. The group member could then wash off the description of the offense, indicating a commitment to forgive. Sometimes the marker does not fully wash off, which can be a picture of forgiveness as a process that unfolds over time rather than as a onetime event.

The fifth step is to *hold on to forgiveness*. Group members might get angry or upset when reminded of an offense that they have previously forgiven. They might feel frustrated and question whether they really forgave. I try to normalize this process for group members. Even though we might try to forgive and forget, remembering and experiencing the emotion related to an offense is normal. I like to use the metaphor of a hot stove; if we have been burned by a hot stove once, we might feel scared or cautious when around one in the future, but it doesn't mean we haven't also experienced healing from the burn. Some strategies to help group members hold on to forgiveness include

- Getting out of the situation that triggered the memory
- Distracting yourself
- Remembering that the pain of the hurt is not the same thing as unforgiveness
- Seeking reassurance and support from others
- Reading over the documents you created in the commit-to-forgive step
- Working through the REACH steps again

Following Edward's apology to Beth, I turned to Beth and asked her how she was feeling about her relationship with

Edward. "Better than when I got to group today," Beth said. I asked her about forgiveness, and whether that was something she might want to explore in her relationship with Edward. "I think forgiveness would be a good thing for me to do," Beth said, "But it's difficult for me." Beth then did some work around why forgiveness was hard for her. She said that Edward seemed really sincere. I invited her to say that to him. So she spoke directly to Edward and shared that he seemed really sincere and that she felt tender toward him and his struggles with his dad. It made sense to her that he struggled with criticism. (Here is where empathy is so helpful. Beth was able to see that his criticism was more about him and less about her.) However, she had been hurt so many times before with so many people that she wasn't sure she could really forgive him. He might hurt her again.

Forgiveness can be a powerful intervention, but I never want to pressure group members to forgive. Beth needed more time to be able to truly offer the gift of forgiveness. She was too hurt to just jump in and do so. But she seemed willing to work on the third step of REACH, offering the altruistic gift of forgiveness, and that was an important step. Hopefully, there would be an opportunity to keep the process going in subsequent groups. Also, linking with others in the group was helpful because she wasn't alone in having difficulty trusting Edward. Other group members had work to do as Edward's criticism had affected them as well.

Reconciliation

Forgiveness and reconciliation are two different things. Forgiveness involves an internal change in one's thoughts, feelings, emotions, and behaviors toward a person who hurts you, whereas reconciliation involves taking steps to repair trust in the relationship (Worthington, 2006). Some people confuse forgiveness and reconciliation or treat them as the same thing, which is problematic for two reasons. First, it can make forgiveness more difficult. People might be ready to forgive, but they may not feel ready to rebuild trust in the relationship. In this case, conflating forgiveness and reconciliation could hinder a person from doing the part of the work they are ready to do. Second, in some situations, reconciliation might be dangerous or impossible. For example, if a person was in a physically abusive relationship, that person might benefit from working through forgiveness, but reengaging in the abusive relationship would not be advisable or safe. Also, people are sometimes in situations where reconciliation is impossible. For example, if a person is struggling with unforgiveness toward a stranger or a family member who has died, reconciliation might be impossible, but forgiveness might be an important step in that person's process of healing and growth.

In many cases, however, reconciliation is an important goal. In fact, for many individuals, part of the purpose of forgiveness is to help lead to repairing a damaged relationship. This is often the case when a conflict or hurt involves the relationship between two group members. Part of the goal of forgiveness is to help repair the relationship between the two group members and rebuild cohesion in the group.

Two main strategies help group members work toward reconciliation. First, trust is rebuilt as time passes without additional offenses. One difficult thing about reconciliation is that it takes time. The victim needs to have some evidence that the other person has changed and also needs some time to know that it is safe to reengage with the person without a high risk of being hurt again. The time that passes without additional offenses can be thought of as boards rebuilding a bridge of trust between two group members.

Second, trust is rebuilt through positive, supportive experiences between group members. John Gottman conducted some research on couples showing that happy and stable couples needed at least five positive experiences to counteract the effects of one negative experience (Gottman & Levenson, 1992). The bad is stronger than the good (Baumeister, Bratslavsky, Finkenauer, & Vohs, 2001), which is why it is so important to address conflict in your group and work through it in a healthy way. This process of working through conflict helps lessen its negative impact on relationships between group members. Still, conflict occurs, and your group members inevitably hurt one another. Encouraging positive, supportive interactions can help build strong relationships between group members and in the process of reconciliation.

Following Beth's work on forgiveness, I asked Beth and Edward if there was anything else they felt like they needed from one another moving forward. Both Edward and Beth expressed that they appreciated being able to work through the conflict rather than sweep it under the rug, like they usually did in their own lives. Beth noted that she still was struggling with some angry feelings toward Edward, but that she definitely wanted to move forward and start rebuilding the trust between them. She noted that it would take time for her to experience Edward as trustworthy. He really would have to stop the criticism. She couldn't keep getting hurt by his words and expect her to just take it and

forgive. I affirmed her comments, and I reminded them that reconciliation and rebuilding trust is a process that takes time. One
final exercise I did was to have Edward and Beth think about
one thing they appreciated about each other, regarding the work
they had just completed. Beth shared that she appreciated that
Edward was so open about exploring his own part in the conflict.
She really appreciated that he took responsibility for his part
when apologizing and trying to make amends. Edward shared
that he appreciated that Beth was so gracious toward him, even
when he didn't deserve it.

Behavior Change Skills

Changing a behavior is difficult. Remember at the beginning
of the chapter I asked you to think about a time you tried to
change a behavior but failed, and how difficult and disheartening
that was. Imagine what you needed from others when you were
struggling with change. I imagine that, at some level, you needed
grace. Your group members need grace as well as they try (and
sometimes fail) to work toward repentance and put the ownership of their truth into action. This process isn't simple or easy.

You can develop certain skills as a group leader to help your
group members work toward repentance and behavior change,
inside and outside the group. These strategies are easy to remember because they all begin with the letter *s*.

Surroundings

The first strategy for helping group members change their behavior is to adjust the *surroundings* to accommodate as much as
possible the change they want to make. For example, if a group

member wants to stop drinking alcohol, it's important to make the environment as accommodating as possible. This means getting rid of all the alcohol in the house and avoiding places where alcohol is present and accessible (e.g., bars and office parties). You want the environment to work for you, rather than against you.

Small

The second strategy is to start *small*. People motivated to change a particular behavior often bite off more than they can chew. They may stick to their plan for a couple of days, but the change was so big that it wasn't sustainable over time. It's better to start small with something you know you can accomplish. Then, after that small change becomes a consistent habit, you can start increasing the degree of change. For example, a group member who wants to begin exercising might try to run five miles on the first day—too big of a change. Instead, you might encourage the group member to start by trying to run for five minutes. This goal is more manageable, and probably something the group member can accomplish. Once the group member has succeeded in running for five minutes, you might suggest increasing to six minutes, with the goal of increasing slowly over time.

Specific

The third strategy is to be *specific*. Group members sometimes have a broad and vague goal, such as "improving my relationship with my wife." This kind of goal is too vague because it's difficult to know whether the goal has been met or not. There aren't easy markers to determine whether the goal was accomplished.

Instead, encourage your group members to set specific goals for themselves. For example, the group member who wanted to improve his relationship with his wife might set a goal to take his wife on a date this Friday night, or write his wife a note on Monday telling her three things that he appreciates about her. Specific behavior changes are more likely to be successful than vague behavior changes.

Schedule

The fourth strategy is to *schedule* it in. Changing any type of behavior feels unnatural at first. You might want it to just be part of your routine, but the reality is that it takes a long time to build a new habit. Research has shown that it takes a little over two months to form a new habit (Lally, van Jaarsveld, Potts, & Wardle, 2010). That's a long time. To get through the two months before a behavior change feels natural, you need to schedule in the change like you would a meeting or appointment. I remember when my wife and I were trying to teach our son to complete his bedtime routine (brushing his teeth, etc.). At first, we had to put a checklist by the bathroom mirror with the bedtime tasks, and my son would check off each task as he completed it. (His weekly allowance was dependent upon him completing all the tasks.) He needed the schedule in order to complete his bedtime routine, because it wasn't a habit yet. But over time, the bedtime routine became natural to him, and he was able to complete it without his checklist. (I am happy to report that my son is now all grown up and still brushes his teeth twice per day.) It is the same way with your group members who are trying to make a behavior change. At first, they need to put the change into their schedule. Over time, it becomes a habit.

Support

The fifth strategy is to find a *support* team. Changing a behavior all by yourself is difficult. We need a community of people supporting us in our change efforts. We weren't meant to do life alone. This lesson was hard for me, because I had a tendency to isolate, but over time I learned that I was much more successful in putting ownership of my truth into action if I had a group of men supporting and checking up on me. One of the most helpful parts of group is the ready-made support system in place for each of your group members. Group members can make commitments in group and hold each other accountable for those commitments. Group members can lean on each other for support, inside and outside the group.

In my group, I implemented the 5 s's in working with Edward on his goal to be less critical and more affirming of the other group members, as well as his wife and children. To adjust the *surroundings*, it was important to consistently enforce the group's ground rule of no judgments. Edward committed to let himself be "caught" whenever he said something that was critical, both in group and at home. He even gave his sons permission to call him out on being critical. Whenever he said something critical, family members would call out, "No judgments." Edward also posted sticky notes around his home and office that reminded him to affirm the people in his life whom he cared about. In this way, Edward's environment was working with him in pursuing his goal, rather than against him.

Starting *small* was important for Edward in his goal to affirm rather than criticize the people in his life. Edward recognized that becoming a more affirming person would be difficult for him and would probably take time. Edward knew that he wasn't going to change overnight. Affirmation was not a part of his experience growing up, but he could learn and grow. So Edward started out small. He agreed to give Jane and his two sons one affirmation per day for the next week. Edward committed to reporting back to the group the following week about how it went.

Agreeing to give Jane and his two sons one affirmation per day was a good start in outlining a goal that was *specific*. In group, I worked with Edward to get even more specific about what kinds of things he could affirm. For example, Edward began by affirming behaviors that Jane and his sons would do (e.g., cook dinner and finish chores). I challenged Edward to also think about how he could affirm aspects of Jane and their sons' character that he appreciated. In a similar way, we worked to be more specific about the kinds of criticism Edward was trying to avoid. By outlining what Edward could affirm specifically in his family members, and what specific criticisms Edward was committing to stop, it would be easier to gauge how Edward was progressing toward his goal.

I then worked with Edward to *schedule* in his affirmations. Edward committed to share his affirmation with Jane every day after he came home from work. They would have a check-in time where he would affirm her. Scheduling affirmations with his boys was more difficult, because both were busy with sports and other after-school activities. He decided that he would do his affirmation on the weekend for his sons. It would be unrealistic right now for him to do the affirmation practice daily, so he decided to start small and affirm his sons weekly. He still committed to affirm Jane daily.

The final *s* was *support.* I checked in with Edward about who could support him in his commitment. Our small group was the main source of support. Each group member agreed to check in with Edward the following week to see how the week went in regard to refraining from judging and instead affirming his wife and sons. What about during the week? Jane said that she would commit to having the check-in with Edward each day, to help him set aside a time that they could affirm one another. Jane also said that she would try her best to give a signal if she noticed Edward making a judgment or criticism around the house. Finally, Ted offered to call Edward on Saturday to check in with him about how the week was going, and remind him about his commitment to affirm his sons on the weekend. Edward had a strong support team in place.

Skills for Working with Setbacks

Setbacks are a normal part of trying to change a behavior. Sometimes we think of setbacks as a failure or as evidence that we really can't make the change. Group leaders can also get discouraged and feel that they are doing something wrong when their group members experience setbacks. You might think that if you were a better leader or did something differently, your group members wouldn't be struggling so much.

But remember how difficult it was to change something in your own life? It's tough to make a change and maintain it, even if you are doing everything right. It's important to remember that perfection isn't the goal. Perfection is impossible, and striving for perfection may make it less likely to successfully change a behavior because it sets people up for failure. Instead of striving for perfection, it's more important to remember that setbacks are a normal part of the change process. For example, many smokers make repeated attempts at quitting before attaining long-term success. Since setbacks are normal, you need to consider how to deal with them when they occur in your small group.

I have three main suggestions for dealing with setbacks. First, *engage with grace* . The group member who had a setback is probably already feeling bad about what happened. Common emotions that co-occur with setbacks include guilt, shame, embarrassment, and despair. The group member having the setback may even try to hide it from the group, fearing what you or the other group members would think. To bring the group member back into the group process with grace, validate the group member for sharing the setback, even though it was probably difficult. Commend the group member for bringing the setback into the light, instead of hiding it in shame. We all experience setbacks, and we all need grace. Encourage other group members to give grace as well.

Second, *explore the setback.* Group members can do work around a setback, which may actually lead to deep work that makes future change efforts more likely. Ask the group member if there is willing to do some work around the setback, and if so, explore the setback in group. Setbacks don't occur in a vacuum. What was happening in the group member's life that led to the setback? What was the group member feeling before it happened? If the group member can identify markers or precursors to the setback, the person may be better able to look out for these triggers in the future, and be better able to prevent further setbacks.

Third, *come up with a plan*. If the group member experienced a new insight when exploring the setback, incorporate it into future change efforts. If a precursor to the setback was identified, the group member could come up with a plan to avoid the precursor in the future. It is also helpful to incorporate relationship support into the plan. In my sex addiction groups, we have a saying, "Reach Out or Act Out" (Hook, Hook, & Hines, 2008). The meaning is that if group members don't reach out to one another for support and help, they probably won't be able to make the change they want. Group members can lean on each other to help each other move forward toward their goal.

When Edward returned to group the following week after committing to affirm rather than criticize and judge his wife and sons, he shared a setback. He did affirm his wife throughout the week during their check-ins, but he also had a major fight with his family that involved Edward yelling at Jane in front of their sons and calling her a name. Following this outburst, Jane left the house for the evening. Edward felt shame about what he did, but this is what happened, and we needed to address it in the group.

When Edward shared the setback about his fight with his wife, I first offered him grace. I said that I appreciated the courage he had to show up to the small group after such a tough week. I honored him for his honesty in continuing to bring his struggles to the group. I told him I felt grace toward him, and that this was a group for struggling people (myself included). Other group members chimed in and offered support and grace as well. They affirmed him for his vulnerability and courage to be honest about what happened.

After giving grace, I asked Edward if he was willing to explore the setback. He said that he was. Edward then did some work about what led up to the setback. The main focus was on one night during the week in which Edward had "lost it" and yelled at and criticized Jane, causing her to leave the house for most of the night. Edward noted a few things that led up to the outburst, including struggling to connect with Jane over the past two days, as well as a difficult day at work.

After exploring the setback, we talked about having a plan moving forward. Edward brainstormed ways that he could avoid taking out his stress on his wife in the future. Also, one change Edward wanted to make was being okay with taking a time-out with Jane if he felt himself getting too heated. Edward and Jane agreed that a time-out would mean that they would take a temporary break, with a commitment to return to the conversation at a later time.

A key to success in helping people work through behavior change and setbacks is to use the group skills addressed earlier in this book. In these situations, I want to bring in the rest of the group whenever possible. For example, I started by encouraging Edward to pick someone to work with, so that he would be in relationship with the other group members throughout the process. Linking allowed other group members to connect with Edward, assuring him that he was not alone in his work. Not everyone experiences the same setbacks that Edward experienced, but everyone does have setbacks, leaders included. Edward's work was everyone's work.

In addition to having the group support Edward in his setback, group members could also challenge Edward on his behavior and the disconnect between his verbal commitment in group and his actions during the week. Group members could reaffirm their commitment to accountability and helping Edward work toward his stated goals in group. Since Edward's wife, Jane, is also in the group, and Edward's setback negatively affected Jane, it would also be important for the group members to support Jane. This support likely involves listening, validation, and empathy, but it may also involve supporting Jane in her own personal work. For example, Jane has been working on becoming more assertive and setting and maintaining boundaries for the kinds of behavior that are not acceptable to her and her family. The group could support her in those goals as she navigates her relationship with Edward.

REPENTANCE EXERCISE: INDIVIDUAL

If you are currently leading a group, reflect on how your small group is going. When your group members take ownership of their issues and growth edges, how are you doing at encouraging them to put ownership of their truth into action, inside and outside the group? How are you doing with helping group members repair their relationships after conflict? Are you helping group members to confess their sin and struggles, not only to God but also to each other? When conflict has occurred in your group, are you facilitating apologies between group members that involve all parts of a complete apology? Once an apology occurs, how are you doing at helping group members forgive one another?

Can you lead group members through the five steps to REACH forgiveness? How are you doing at bringing all the group members into the process of forgiveness?

_____

_____

_____

What about behavior change? How are you doing at helping group members turn away from their old way of behaving and taking concrete steps in the direction they want to go? When group members are working on the changes they want to make in their lives, inside and outside of group, are you encouraging them to follow the five *s*'s of effective behavior change? Are group members adjusting their *surroundings*, starting *small*, being *specific*, *scheduling* it in, and using their *support* team? How do you respond when group members have setbacks? Are you using your linking skills to bring the rest of the group members into the process?

_____

_____

_____

Reflect on your abilities to help your group members put ownership of their truth into action via repentance. Which of these skills are you good at? Which of these skills do you need to work on? Pick a skill and commit to practicing it. Write down your growth edge for repentance.

_____

_____

_____

REPENTANCE EXERCISE: GROUP

If you are working through this book as part of a training with other readers, complete these two exercises focused on helping group members put ownership of their truth into action through repentance.

The first exercise involves helping group members repair a relationship following a conflict. Pick one person to be the group leader and two people to be group members with the conflict. One group member plays the offender, and one group member plays the victim. The offender gives the victim a brief apology (e.g., "Sorry about that"). The group leader picks one aspect of making an effective apology and coaches the offender about how to give a more effective apology using the chosen aspect. Then the group leader picks one of the five steps to REACH forgiveness and leads the victim through an exercise designed to help with the chosen step. Finally, the group leader works with both group members to identify one positive interaction they could have in order to begin to rebuild trust and work toward reconciliation. Repeat this exercise until each person has had a chance to be the group leader.

The second exercise involves helping group members to create an effective plan for behavior change using the five *s*'s. Pair up within your group. Pick one person to be the group leader and one person to be the group member. The group members share a behavior that they would like to change. The group leaders ask the group members to think of a step to work toward that behavior change. The group members think of a step that violates one of the five *s*'s (e.g., huge first step, vague plan). The group leaders work with the group members to come up with a revised step that is in line with the five *s*'s.

Back to Grace

HEALING AND GROWTH are lifelong processes. Of course, individuals might go through seasons where their personal work is more intensive or less intensive. People might take breaks from deep personal work in order to focus on other aspects of their life, but I don't think the work of healing and personal growth ever ends. In my own life, I want to be continually growing, changing, and learning. The moment I stop doing that or give up on that process, I start to feel numb or even dead inside.

I believe the same is true of your group members. That's why The Healing Cycle is designed to be ongoing. It's not something you go through once and then are done but is a process that leads to deeper levels of healing and growth over time. When group members begin their process, they likely are experiencing just a small amount of grace and safety, despite your best efforts as group leader to set this foundation. The first time group members share, they probably just scratch the surface in regard to their level of vulnerability, as well as the depth of truth they are open to owning and repenting of. This first time around The Healing Cycle, however, leads to a deeper experience of grace, which in turn leads to increased feelings of safety, increased vulnerability, and a greater depth of truth that leads to more ownership and repentance.

Although I believe healing and growth are continuous and life-long processes, most groups that you lead end at some point. You may even be leading a group that is time-limited. From the outset, you may plan to meet for a specified number of meetings (e.g., ten sessions) or a specified length of time (e.g., three months). In the marriage support groups I help out with at church, couples sign up for a group that meets for nine weeks. The group begins and ends on specific dates. After the nine weeks are finished, there is a break before the next opportunity to sign up for the group.

On the other hand, you might lead a small group that is open-ended. My therapy groups for men struggling with sexual addiction are open-ended. Men commit at the outset to be part of the group for at least six months, but after that commitment, they decide for themselves how long they want to stay. If you lead an open-ended group, most group members decide to leave the group at some point, and for various reasons. A group member might get a new job and leave the area, for example, or a group member might feel like enough progress has been made and the support is no longer needed. Other group members might just feel as if they need to take a break. Still other members might feel that the group process isn't working for them and they want to quit. It can be challenging for group leaders when group members want to leave, especially if the group leader doesn't feel that the group member is ready to go.

Psychology, the Healing Process, and Ending Well

Across theories of psychology, termination is an important phase of treatment that tends to involve several key tasks (Joyce, Piper, Ogrodniczuk, & Klein, 2007). First, people need a chance to integrate their experiences in the group, including positive and negative feelings about their work. Group members have a chance to tell a story about how they have grown, where they still hope to grow, and how they will integrate what they have learned in group into their life going forward. This process consolidates the progress made in treatment.

In addition, ending well often involves saying thank-you. When people perceive that others (e.g., the group leader and other group members) have given them a gift, honoring that gift deepens the connection and is an expression of gratitude. Group members have a chance to make the connections they formed a permanent part of their life moving forward.

Finally, ending well involves saying good-bye. Group members need a chance to express the variety of feelings associated with the transition in the relationships. In some contexts, such as group therapy, they may not see the leader or other group members again. In other contexts, such as a church small group, the nature of the relationships changes even though people will see other group members again.

How psychologists view termination depends on the degree to which the group is time-limited or open-ended. Some counselors prefer counseling to be time-limited. Time-limited counseling is often used when the problem is more specific, like a phobia.

Researchers have developed specific kinds of interventions for specific types of problems, and these programs often are time-limited and specify a certain number of sessions. There are some benefits to providing a structure on the amount of time that counseling will take. Because of the time limit, there is a need for sessions to be more organized and focused, which can help the counselor and client stay on track. There can be a greater emphasis on clients internalizing the work of counseling and becoming their own counselor, instead of relying on another person.

Other counselors prefer counseling to be open-ended. Open-ended counseling is often used when the problem is more general or has to do with one's relationships or aspects of one's personality. Open-ended counseling often explores what is happening in the here and now but also tries to connect one's current problems with the person's history or family of origin. There are also benefits to open-ended counseling. Clients and counselors don't feel rushed. There is ample time to explore issues and problems. The relationship between the counselor and client has enough time to grow, develop, and work through ruptures. Open-ended counseling may fit better with the idea that healing and growth represent a lifelong process rather than a particular endpoint.

Throughout this chapter, we discuss some issues related to both types of groups. Irrespective of whether a course of counseling is time-limited or open-ended, almost all psychologists place a high level of importance on the termination process when ending a counseling relationship. Clients often forge strong and deep bonds with their counselors, and ending those relationships well can be difficult. In group therapy, when a group member leaves a group or the group disbands, the procedures around termination are more complex. Not only are group members ending their relationships with the group leader, but they are also ending their relationships with each other. Group leaders need to help group members end well.

CHRISTIANITY, THE HEALING PROCESS, AND ENDING WELL

The Christian faith uses various metaphors and stories to describe the process of healing, growth, and ending well. The Old Testament is full of stories about great leaders and their ups and downs in their walks with God. For example, Abraham, the man with whom God created his initial covenant, struggled with fear, lied about his wife, and gave her to be with another man in order to save his own skin (Genesis 20). God stuck with him. Moses, the man God picked to lead his people out of slavery, kept trying to get out of his job because he didn't view himself as a good enough speaker (Exodus 4). God stuck with him. David, whom God called a "man after his own heart," committed adultery with Bathsheba and then conspired to kill her husband (2 Samuel 11). God stuck with him. Yet often these leaders did not end well. For example, Moses was not permitted to enter the Promised Land (Numbers 20:12). Often the kings of Israel, like Solomon, King David's son, started out well, but ended poorly (1 Kings 11).

One of my favorite stories in the Bible about the process of healing and growth is the story of Jesus and Peter. Peter definitely had his ups and downs during Jesus' life and ministry. Peter had the boldness to walk on water, but then lost faith in the midst of his fear (Matthew 14:22–36). He was ready to fight for Jesus and cut off the ear of one of the people trying to arrest him, but Peter failed to understand that Jesus didn't want him to resist with violence (John 18:10–11). Perhaps the low point of Peter's relationship with Jesus occurred when Peter denied three times that he knew Jesus, even though earlier that day he had pledged his loyalty (Luke 22:54–62).

Even after Peter disowns Jesus, Jesus sticks with him. There is a passage in the Gospel of John in which Jesus reinstates Peter (John 21:15–19). Jesus asks Peter three times if Peter loves him. It is a beautiful parallel to Peter's three-part denial. Jesus offers grace to Peter and allows Peter to own the truth about his denial, and Peter repents by confessing his love for Jesus three times, moving forward in a new direction.

The apostle Paul also talks quite a bit about the process of healing and growth, as well as the importance of ending well. Paul uses a race metaphor to describe the process of healing and growth in the spiritual life. In his letter to the church in Corinth, Paul compares the spiritual life to the training of an athlete. "Do you not know that in a race all runners run, but only one gets the prize? Run in such a way as to get the prize. Everyone who competes in the games goes into strict training. They do it to get a crown that will not last, but we do it to get a crown that will last forever. Therefore, I do not run like someone running aimlessly; I do not fight like a boxer beating the air. No, I strike a blow to my body and make it my slave so that after I have preached to others, I myself will not be disqualified" (1 Corinthians 9:24–27). Near the end of his life, Paul reflected on his own process of healing and growth in a letter to Timothy. "For I am already being poured out like a drink offering, and the time for my departure is near. I have fought the good fight, I have finished the race, I have kept the faith" (2 Timothy 4:6–7). In this way, Paul ended well.

THE HEALING PROCESS IN THE GROUP

When your group members do their work, it sets the stage for them to experience deeper levels of grace—from you the group leader; the other group members; and God. This was certainly true one week in group for Ted, the group member who triggered me because he talked too much. The week before, we were talking about that very issue in the group. Edward had confronted Ted for showing off and talking too much in group, and much to my surprise, Ted wasn't defensive. I asked him if he wanted to do some work around this issue, and Ted said that he would.

Ted shared vulnerably, talking about growing up as the youngest of three kids. He described getting picked on by the neighborhood kids, who were all older than him. He shared about having undiagnosed dyslexia, and how the other students would call him stupid. He talked about having to be funny and tell jokes in order to survive. He also shared his experiences with his parents. His dad wasn't around very much, and his mom was preoccupied with the other kids and running the household. He wondered if part of his talking too much and showing off started there as well, trying to get his parents to notice him.

The group felt connected throughout the discussion. James and Jane connected by sharing similar struggles when they were growing up. Ted's wife, Alice, started to cry and said she felt like she understood her husband in a new and deeper way than she ever had. Ted was able to take ownership of his tendency to dominate the conversation in group. He said that he wanted to work on listening more and being more open and available to support the other group members. Ted asked for the group to hold him accountable when he got off track.

An amazing thing happened after Ted did his work in the group. Instead of getting frustrated with Ted, as they had previously, the group members responded with unconditional acceptance. Ted had opened his heart up to the group, and they responded with grace. Throughout the group session that night, I felt my heart warming toward Ted as well, even though Ted was one of the most difficult group members for me to connect with and offer grace. His tendency to talk a lot and show off reminded me of my dad, bringing up a lot of anger and frustration in me. I had a tough time accepting Ted as is. I wanted him to change—right now. I had to do some work around this issue in my own group to be able to engage with Ted as a leader.

But as Ted did his work in the group, I found myself having empathy and compassion for him in a new way. It didn't take as much work for me to offer him a heart of grace; I realized that it was naturally there. After seeing Ted do his own work and express greater vulnerability, I had more patience and understanding for him. As I thanked him for doing his work, I commented on his courage and vulnerability. I told him I felt closer to him and more connected to him than I ever had.

That kind of experience is common in small groups, and it illustrates the reciprocal nature of The Healing Cycle. Grace and safety set the foundation for healing and growth to occur in a small group. With grace and safety in place, group members are able to share vulnerably about their pain and struggles. As group members share more vulnerably, they are more open to receive truth and feedback about their behavior and situation. Group members are then able to take ownership of their truth and put that ownership into action through repentance. As group members repent and seek to move in a new direction, they experience deeper levels of grace from each other, the group leader, and God.

In this final chapter, I want to share some of my thoughts about how the process of healing and growth happens in small groups over time. What does that process look like? How does The Healing Cycle continue and encourage group members to go even deeper? How do you bring in new members to an already existing group? How do you know when group members are done with their work? How do group members end well? I address these questions as I conclude this book.

Continuing the Process of Healing and Growth

One thing that can help group members end well is to connect their experience in group to an ongoing process of growth and change that continues throughout their lives. You can use three helpful skills to reinforce this connection: framing, celebrating, and letting go.

Framing

The first skill is framing. Consider how we as leaders communicate about the process of healing and growth. Group members may enter the group with various ideas about how the process will go, or what it looks like for them to "get better." Some group members may think that you as the group leader are there to fix them. Others may think that they just need to learn a new skill or understand something about their past, and then they will change. Still other group members might spiritualize the process of healing and growth, believing that they just need to get closer to God or learn more about the Bible in order to change.

Language is important. Come up with a metaphor or story for how you view the process of healing and growth. I like the metaphor of a journey, which has several helpful aspects. First, a journey takes time. The process of healing and growth usually isn't a quick fix. Second, a journey has different stages. Sometimes the process of healing and growth is really intense, and other times are periods of rest. Third, a journey is more rewarding when done with others. Healing and growth happen best in the context of community. Fourth, the joy is often in the journey itself, rather than in the destination. The process of healing and growth often becomes rewarding in and of itself, as opposed to realizing a particular goal or achievement. The metaphor isn't perfect, but it works for me.

Think about how you view the process of healing and growth. Is there a metaphor that captures how you think about this process? Write down one metaphor that rings true with you and why. Feel free to use it when framing the process of your group members.

Celebrating

A second leader skill for continuing the growth process is celebrating and encouraging group members' progress. Group members have unique personalities, personal histories, and methods of presentation. Group members also have a unique pace for their progress in a small group. In some situations you may not be aware of the internal process and healing that are occurring inside group members. You may feel that a group member has made a small step (e.g., exhibiting a small bit of vulnerability), but this step could feel massive for the group member. Celebrate and encourage the steps group members take, no matter how small they may seem on the surface. Remember to bring in the other group members to help you celebrate a group member's growth, because such encouragement is even more effective when group members praise one another.

Letting Go

A third leader skill for helping group members view healing and growth as a lifelong process is to hold the progress of group members with a loose grip, letting group members control their own process. Group leaders sometimes feel responsible for their group members' progress. Leaders may feel frustrated or upset if group members do not make as much progress as anticipated or decide to leave the group. Remember that group members are responsible for their own lives, including their own process of healing and growth. Even if group members do not improve as much as the group leader would like, the group leader must learn to accept it. Maybe the group member has completed a piece of his work and will return to continue the process at a later time. The more that group leaders can let go of control over their group members' process, the more effective they will be as leaders.

Ending Well

All small groups eventually come to an end. Ending a small group can be a complex process, and doing it well can be difficult. In this section, I address several issues that often come up when small groups come to an end, including poor endings, ending well in open-ended groups, bringing in new group members, ending well in time-limited groups, and asking group members to leave.

Poor Endings

There are a variety of ways that group members can end their work poorly, which can undermine gains achieved during participation in the group. For example, a common occurrence is for a group member to simply quit the small group without saying good-bye. You may have had questions when this happened: Why did that person leave? Did the member not like the group? Did the member not like me? Was I doing a bad job as a leader?

Having members leave can make me doubt my own work. Group members have similar questions and feelings when someone leaves unannounced, even if they haven't surfaced in the group yet.

Our small groups are microcosms of our lives. This difficulty of ending a small group well reflects a deeper problem that we often have as human beings in relationship with one another. In our everyday lives, we rarely end relationships well. Think back on your own relationships and how they ended. What was that experience like for you? What process did you go through when you ended a relationship? Did you have a process? What feelings came up for you when you ended a relationship?

_____

_____

_____

When I was young, I felt like I had a lot of unsettled endings in my relationships. Because my parents were missionaries, I grew up going to boarding schools. Since missionary families came and went, at the end of every school year, a round of ending relationships took place, and I wasn't sure if I would ever see my friends again. When I was in sixth grade, I was the one who moved—to the United States to go to boarding school. More endings. I didn't really know how to deal with these endings or cope with my own feelings about them. What happened is that I didn't address the endings or the feelings that accompanied them. Sometimes I just tried to slip away when an ending was looming, not even saying good-bye.

Think about other times you have exited a relationship or situation. What about your work life? When you changed jobs for different opportunities, did you feel like you ended well? What about the other side of the coin? Have you ever been fired? Did you feel like your boss or supervisor ended well with you, even though the situation was not what you wanted? What about the deaths you have experienced? Did you end well with loved ones who have passed away? Were you able to say good-bye, connect, and receive closure around the death of a loved one? What comes to mind when you think about your other experiences exiting situations or ending relationships?

_____

_____

_____

Some of our deepest hurts involve poor endings. Ending well is hard, so almost all of us, leaders and group members alike, have at least some unfinished business from lost relationships. Because of prior patterns of dealing with loss, your group members need help to end well. As a result, how members finish a group provides them with a powerful opportunity to experience integration and healing around prior losses.

Ending Well in Open-Ended Groups

I work hard to end my groups well. For example, in my therapy groups, as part of the ground rules of the group, I ask that when group members decide to leave, they give the group at least a month's notice. A month is about how long it takes to adequately work through issues of leaving and ending relationships. I use the guideline of a month so that the group member who is leaving can end well, tie up loose ends, and say good-bye. Also, the other group members can have a good experience of ending their relationships with the group member who is leaving. Obviously, some group members may not follow this guideline. I often have to remind members of this commitment when they decide to leave.

When a group member decides to leave, it brings up all sorts of reactions, both in the group member who is leaving as well as with the other group members. Many group members do some of their best work in that final month. Some group members naturally use their entire last month to say good-bye to the group and do work around saying good-bye. I invite group members who leave to give other group members feedback on their experience. I also invite group members to give the person leaving their feedback as well. The experience is often very positive. If the group member waits until the last day to start saying final good-byes, I intentionally focus the group on saying good-bye for most of the last session rather than just easing out of the group without some kind of process. For example, I might say, "I notice we haven't talked a lot about the fact that today is _____'s last day. This is really on my mind right now. I wonder what you want to do tonight to end well?"

Other types of groups, such as church support groups, may also be open-ended, with a continual flow of people coming in and out. These types of support groups generally have less structure than therapy groups. Participants pay to show up for therapy groups, so the members don't often slide out so easily. With support groups, however, it can be more difficult to provide a context for ending well. It is often easy for group members to just miss a few weeks and then never return.

For support groups, it is important to create boundaries around attendance and missing group sessions. For example, I ask group members to tell me when they will miss, and I make sure that a system is in place to call the missing group member after a week or two. Similarly, it is important to make it a value and a requirement to have an ending session where the group member can say good-bye, rather than just missing a couple sessions and never coming back. The key, even in these less structured groups, is to have explicit boundaries around attendance as well as the ending process. You may want to use the one-month guideline that I use in my therapy groups. If this isn't feasible for the type of group you lead, perhaps you can lower the requirement to one or two weeks. At a minimum, however, have a boundary that group members must have a time to end well and say good-bye in the group.

No matter how hard you try to create boundaries around ending well, group members sometimes leave without saying good-bye and do not follow your guidelines. This can be frustrating for the group leader, and the group leader and group members may have questions or feelings about the group member who has left. Process these questions and feelings in the group and explore their meanings for group members. For example, having a group member leave could trigger past experiences of loss and unhappy endings in your group members' lives. This can actually be helpful work to engage during the group. In the end, do what you can to help create a context where group members can end well, but remember that you ultimately cannot control group members' actions and behaviors.

Bringing in New Group Members

In open-ended groups, when group members leave, you may decide to introduce new members in order to maintain a helpful group size. Groups that have fewer than four or more than ten members often have difficulties maintaining strong cohesion. Integrating new group members brings up several important challenges or questions. How can you incorporate a new group member without disrupting the cohesion that has been built in your group over time? How can you bring the new group member up to speed without repeating everything you discussed at the beginning of the group? Although bringing in new members always has some challenges, it also presents an opportunity for growth as group members learn to maintain a culture of grace even as the group shifts over time.

A good idea is to meet with potential group members individually before introducing them into the group. The purpose of this individual meeting is to assess whether the potential members are ready for group, and to let them know the boundaries and ground rules of the group (see chapter 3). I ask any potential new group members whether they understand the ground rules and are willing to commit to them.

I always tell the small group in advance that we have a new member coming. (In my therapy group, I also say the name of the new group member, to see if any existing group members know the individual or have a problem with the new group member attending the group. If any existing group members know the potential group member, it may be better for both parties if they attend different groups.) After making the announcement about the new group member, I let the group work through any issues they may have with bringing in a new member. For example, I remember leading a group in which an existing group member didn't want a new group member to join, because the member was in a tough place and didn't want someone new taking up more of the group time. I provided space for the existing group member to share his feelings and receive support from the other group members.

It is important to have a process to bring the new person into the group. For example, I like to start my groups with a check-in, in which all group members share how they are feeling (SASHET: sad, angry, scared, happy, excited, tender), and then give a brief context for their feeling. So when I bring in a new group member, I might explain what a check-in is, and invite the existing group members to check in first, in order to model the process. Usually the new group member gets a sense of the process after a few group members have modeled.

Another example of a process that can be used to bring new members into the group is to have the existing group members share their answers to two questions: "What brought you to the group in the first place?" and "What is your main work now?" Answering the first question gives the new group member insight into the existing group members' stories. The second question invites existing group members to bring the new group member up to date and identify their current ongoing work. I find this exercise helpful not only for the new group member but also for the existing group members. It can be helpful for existing group members to think about what first brought them to group, as well as how they have experienced healing, growth, and change over the course of the group so far.

After each of the existing group members has shared their answers to the two questions, I invite the new group member to share his story. What brings the person to the small group? What would the new member like to work on in group? What does the person hope to get out of group? After the new group member checks in, I begin to do the leader's work. I invite any existing group member to connect with what the new group member shared. I create a link, and the group process gets started. The new group member learns how the group process works by observation, and often after a few sessions the new group member is fully integrated.

Sometimes, if I have the time, I invite the existing group members to share the boundaries or ground rules of the group. (I make it a point to briefly go over the boundaries with the new group member before joining the group, so these ground rules should not come as a surprise.) This is an important reminder of the boundaries that help create and maintain safety, not only for the new group member, but also for the existing group members. When a new group member comes into the group, the boundaries and ground rules are more caught than taught. Even so, every group member needs to be on the same page with the boundaries and ground rules.

Ending Well in Time-Limited Groups

Time-limited groups, as I've discussed, have a specified start and end date, such as the marriage support groups that my wife and I run in our church. In these groups, all group members end their work in the group at the same time. It is important to help group members with this process of ending, because they likely will not have had a history of ending well in their own relationships. My main recommendation is to come up with a structured process around the group ending. This may feel somewhat artificial or forced, but the reality is that if you as group leader do not come up with a process to help the group members end well, nothing is likely to happen. Group members may just slip out of the group, feeling unfinished about the group process.

Here is an example of a structured process I have used to end my time-limited groups. If you connect with this example, try it in your own group, or feel free to take parts of this example and adjust them to fit your own personal needs and leadership style. You can also come up with something on your own. The important thing is to create a process you can proactively use to help group members end well.

The week before the final session, I invite the group members to write down answers to the following questions to help them end well. I ask two main sets of questions: First, what was your main takeaway from your small group experience? What did you learn about yourself? What will you take with you moving forward? What about you is different now? What is your next step of growth? Second, think about your experiences with each other member of the group during our time together. What positive qualities did you see and experience from each person over the course of group? What did you appreciate most about each person? What will you remember about each person? What about each person will you take with you moving forward?

These two sets of questions give plenty of material for the last session. During the final small group meeting, I put each group member, one at a time, in the "hot seat" and invite the other group members to affirm that group member and voice to that person the "gold" that they see in that person. I invite the group member who is receiving the affirmations to open their hands, work on receiving the gold, and just say, "Thanks." It is a powerful way to end a small group. Also, if we have enough time, I invite group members to share their main takeaway from group. The key to ending well is connecting well. The relationships that are built and developed are among the most important parts of a small group experience. Ending these relationships well prepares group members to enter their next relationship with confidence.

Asking Group Members to Leave

Endings are often joyful times for celebrating the work that was done in group and the relationships that were developed. Some endings, however, are not as fun. One of the most difficult is when you have to ask a group member to leave the group. This occurrence is not common and, depending on your group context, may happen very rarely. Still, it sometimes does happen, and you need to know what to do when this kind of situation arises.

You might need to ask someone to leave the group for two main reasons. The first reason is if the group member needs a different level of care than the group is offering. For example, imagine you are leading an interpersonal process therapy group at a college counseling center. Most of your group members are dealing with mild to moderate psychological symptoms of depression and anxiety, as well as interpersonal difficulties. However, you have one group member who is very depressed and suicidal, and you have become increasingly concerned about the group member's physical safety. It may be that the group is not the right place for that group member, or that individual needs a higher level of care (e.g., individual therapy or hospitalization). A similar situation may come up in recovery or support groups. You might have a group member who needs a higher level of care than can be offered in the group (e.g., individual or group therapy by a licensed professional counselor). In such situations, you need to refer the group member to an appropriate modality and help the group member and group make a good transition after the move.

The second reason you might ask a group member to leave is if the group member fails to keep the commitments of the group and is not responsive to your interventions to help the person stick to the group's boundaries. One common example of a broken commitment is failure to attend group consistently. In order for the group to feel safe, group members need to show up consistently. A group member who struggles with consistent attendance poses difficulties for him- or herself as well as the rest of the group. Stories might surface around the group member who is not showing up, such as, "He doesn't care," "She's not committed," "He doesn't want to work," "She isn't safe." Such stories can damage the group process, as decreased safety might cause others to be less open in their own sharing and work.

If you think you need to ask a group member to leave, I recommend a four-step process. The first step is to consult with a supervisor or colleague. It can be difficult for a group member who is asked to leave a group, and the process is not easy. For this reason, get a second opinion from a supervisor or colleague whom you trust. Check in and see if the supervisor or colleague views the situation in the same way. Is there anything about your own past or history this group member is triggering? Is the decision to ask the group member to leave sound and based on evidence? Have you tried to intervene to help the group member to the extent you are able? In addition to connecting with a supervisor or colleague to get a second opinion, you as the group leader should have support as you go through the process.

The second step is to meet with the group member individually to discuss your concerns, but before making a final decision about the member's future with the group. This conversation could be helpful in understanding the group member's perspective, as well as explaining in detail why the group member is being asked to leave. The conversation might even lead to a new or different solution that you had not considered previously. Before having an individual meeting with the group member, though, address the issue in group. Group members should not be surprised by the meeting. A guideline that I have about conflict is that group members need to work out their conflicts in the group rather than outside of it. If issues surface in the group but are dealt with outside the group, the group misses out on working through the issue. I use the same guideline when asking a group member to leave the group.

The third step is to bring the ending back into the group as a whole. The best-case scenario is to have the leaving group member present, so the whole group (including the group member who is leaving) can process and share their feelings about the situation. Having the group member present also allows the group member who is leaving, as well as the entire group, to say goodbye, seek closure, and end well. Sometimes having the presence of the group member who is leaving is not possible. Group members may be too angry or hurt by being asked to leave. That member may refuse to come back to the group for a final session. In these situations, still discuss the situation in the group with the remaining group members and provide a context for the remaining members to share their thoughts and feelings.

The fourth and final step is to connect the group member who is leaving with necessary referrals and resources. It is often disconcerting for a group member to be asked to leave a group. The small group may have been one of the person's only sources of support and relationship. Don't leave group members to fend for themselves. Connect the group member who is leaving with referrals and resources for individual or group therapy, or other types of support groups.

Example of Working Through Endings

When James left my group, it was an example of a difficult ending. James left group after he and Alice got into a conflict. James felt like Alice was judging him and spiritualizing his problems. Both got angry. I tried to work through it in group as best I could, but it was a struggle, and James did not return the following week. This wasn't the first time James had missed group without letting someone know, but this time he didn't return the following week either. I tried calling him, but he did not return my phone calls or those of other group members. He was gone. Ideally, James would have returned, and we could have worked through the conflict in the group. But since James did not return, we didn't have that opportunity.

Even though I wasn't able to work through the conflict with James, I wanted to make sure the rest of the group had the opportunity to process James's leaving. To start things off, I asked group members to share if and how James's leaving triggered them. Lots of stories surfaced around their own poor endings. Edward shared about a time when he fired one of his long-term employees. There wasn't much of a process around the firing; Edward just told his employee to gather his things and walked him out of the office that day. The employee didn't have a chance to say good-bye to anyone. Edward felt sad and was reminded of how his harshness had hurt others. He could have made an excuse for himself, because that was just how things were done in his business, but he took ownership and reaffirmed his commitment to do things differently. James's leaving gave Edward a chance to do his own work and reinforce the healing that was happening in his life.

Alice probably had the most difficulty with James leaving, because she was most closely involved in the conflict that led it. Alice started to cry and shared that she felt like it was her fault that James left the group. The rest of the group listened to Alice and offered support. Jane noted that each person in the group was responsible for their own work, including James. I tried to strike a balance with Alice. Echoing what Jane shared, I encouraged her not to take responsibility for another person's work. I said that I didn't think it was her fault that James left; James was responsible for himself. I also asked Alice if she could take anything with her moving forward from her conflict with James. Alice thought about it and shared that when she sees someone struggling, like James, her pull is to take care of him. Others sometimes experience this as controlling and spiritualizing. Alice said she felt a new commitment to focus on her own work in group, and not to try to control others.

As you can see from this example, having a group member leave is not only a great learning opportunity for the person who is leaving to do some work, but also for others (including the leader) to do some work around endings. What gets triggered for the other group members when a group member leaves? What gets triggered for you as the leader when a group member leaves, especially if you believe that the person's work is not yet done? When a group member wants to leave, a crisis is created, and the door is open for people to do some of their best work. Sometimes what happens in a group isn't as important as what you do with what happens there.

Our Own Ending: Encouragement and Send-Off

Just as small groups have endings, this book is coming to an end. In this last section, I hope to reiterate the key themes of the book, give you a chance to integrate what you have learned, and think about your own continued journey of growth as a group leader. My hope is that by reading this book, you can go forward better prepared to lead the members of your small group in their process of healing and growth. As you move forward, remember to give yourself grace. Just as your group members have a process of healing and growth, you have your own process as a group leader. If you are just starting out, leading can sometimes be a struggle. You may wonder if you have what it takes to be a good leader. Keep at it. Connect yourself with others who are leading groups so that you can have a support team in place. Find a supervisor or coach who can help you with your questions and concerns about leading groups. Don't worry too much if you make a mistake. It's part of the process.

In your interactions with your group members, start with grace. When in doubt, err on the side of grace. Life is a struggle. Your group members present with all sorts of pain and brokenness. Sometimes your group members arrive with a problem that you have no idea how to address. When in doubt, give your group members grace, love, support, and acceptance, and help your group members learn to do the same for each other. I am continually amazed at the power of grace to heal pain and brokenness.

Work hard to keep your groups safe. Set up your boundaries and ground rules at the beginning and stick with them. It might feel artificial to present the boundaries and block boundary violations when they occur, but be persistent about sticking with the boundaries. You are creating a container in which your group members can do their work. Every time you reinforce the boundaries, or block boundary violations, you make the container more secure. Your group members can feel this, even if they aren't aware of what exactly is happening. If you can't do anything else, focus on building a foundation of grace and safety in your groups.

Once the foundation of grace and safety is set, the magic of the group can begin to happen. It is incredibly healing for people to work out their struggles in the context of relationship. Healing doesn't happen alone. Healing and growth come about in the context of loving, supportive relationships with one another. You as the group leader have the opportunity to be in relationship with your group members, and also to help develop strong supportive relationships between your group members. The foundation of grace, safety, and relationship sets the stage for vulnerable sharing, owning one's truth, and repentance. These experiences in turn lead to deeper experiences of grace.

Continuing the Process and Ending Well Exercise: Individual

If you are currently leading a group, reflect on how your small group is going. How are you doing at helping your group members see their experiences of healing and growth as a process? Do you have a metaphor or framework that you use to help group members reflect on their own process?

_____

_____

_____

How are you doing around controlling your group members'

process? Do you hold their process with a light grip? How do you feel if group members aren't progressing as much or as fast as you would like?

_____

_____

_____

How are you doing when you bring a new group member into an existing group? Do you have a process for integrating the new group member?

_____

_____

_____

What about your experiences with ending well? In your own life, how have endings and exits been for you? Have you been able to end your relationships well, or have the endings been painful?

_____

_____

_____

How do you feel when group members want to end their time

in group? Do you have a process for leading group members through their endings? What about the challenge of asking group members to leave? How do you feel about doing that? If you have asked group members to leave in the past, how has that process gone for you?

_____

_____

_____

Reflect on your skills in helping group members see their work as a process, bringing new members into the group, and helping group members end well. Which of these skills are you good at? Which of these skills do you need to work on? Pick a skill and commit to practicing it. Write down your growth edge for continuing the process and ending well.

_____

_____

_____

Continuing the Process and Ending Well Exercise: Group

If you are working through this book as part of a training with other readers, complete these three exercises focused on helping group members see their work as a process, bringing new members into the group, and ending well.

The first exercise involves helping group members view their healing and growth as a lifelong process. Pick one person to be the group leader, and one person to be the group member. The group member shares an issue. The group leader encourages the group member for the work that has been done, and also briefly shares how healing and growth represent a process that takes time. If time allows, the group leader could briefly share a favorite metaphor for viewing healing and growth as a lifelong process. Repeat this exercise until each person has had a chance to be the group leader.

The second exercise addresses bringing a new member into the group. Pick one person to be the group leader and one person to be the new group member. The group leader picks a process for introducing the new group member into the group—perhaps one of the processes I suggested in this chapter, or you can come up with your own idea. Explain how the process works and lead one existing group member and the new group member through the process. Repeat this exercise until each person has had a chance to be the group leader.

The third exercise involves practicing how to end well. Pick one person to be the group leader and one person to be the group member who is leaving. The group leader takes the group through an ending process. First, the group member who is leaving briefly shares one or two main things learned in group and will take away as the individual moves forward. Second, each other group member briefly shares one piece of gold that they see in the group member who is leaving. This should be encouragement for who the group member is right now, rather than something that the group member "could be if the person worked harder in the future." Be careful that the encouraging messages are actually encouraging for the group member who is leaving. Repeat this exercise until each person has had a chance to be both the group leader and the group member who is leaving.

References

American Psychological Association (2002). Ethical principles of psychologists and code of conduct. *American Psychologist, 57*, 1060–1073.

Baer, R. A. (2006). *Mindfulness-based treatment approaches: Clinician's guide to evidence base and applications.* San Diego, CA: Elsevier Academic Press.

Baumeister, R. F., Bratslavsky, E., Finkenauer, C., & Vohs, K. D. (2001). Bad is stronger than good. *Review of General Psychology, 5*, 323–370.

Beck, A. T. (1976). *Cognitive therapy and the emotional disorders.* Oxford: International Universities Press.

Beck, J. T. (1995). *Cognitive therapy: Basics and beyond.* New York: Guilford Press.

Bernard, H., Burlingame, G., Flores, P., Greene, L., Joyce, A., Kobos, J. C., Leszcz, M., Semands, R. R. M., Piper, W. E., Slocum McEneaney, A. M., & Feirman, D. (2008). Clinical practice guidelines for group psychotherapy. *International Journal of Group Psychotherapy, 58*, 455–542.

Brown, B. (2012). *Daring greatly: How the courage to be vulnerable transforms the way we live, love, parent, and lead.* New York: Avery.

Cannon, W. B. (1932). *The wisdom of the body.* New York: Norton.

Carron, A. V., & Brawley, L. R. (2000). Cohesion: Conceptual and measurement issues. *Small Group Research, 31*, 89–106.

Cheng, C., Cheung, S., Chio, J. H., & Chan, M. S. (2013). Cultural meaning of perceived control: A meta-analysis of locus of control and psychological symptoms across 18 cultural regions. *Psychological Bulletin, 139*, 152–188.

Cloud, H., & Townsend, J. (1992). *Boundaries: When to say yes, how to say no to take control of your life.* Grand Rapids: Zondervan.

Curtis, B., & Eldridge, J. (1997). *The sacred romance: Drawing closer to the heart of God.* Nashville: Edward Nelson.

Egan, G. (1986). *The skilled helper* (3rd ed.). Belmont, CA: Brooks/Cole.

Freud, S. (1915/1961). Instincts and their vicissitudes. In J. Strachey (Ed. and Trans.), *The standard edition of the complete works of Sigmund Freud* (Vol. 14, pp. 111–142). London: Hogarth Press.

Gottman, J. M., & Levenson, R. W. (1992). Marital processes predictive of later dissolution: Behavior, physiology, and health. *Journal of Personality and Social Psychology, 63*, 221–233.

Hayes, S. C., Luoma, J. B., Bond, F. W., Masuda, A., & Lillis, J. (2006). Acceptance and commitment therapy: Model, processes, and outcomes. *Behaviour Research and Therapy, 44*, 1–25.

Hayes, S. C., Masuda, A., Bissett, R., Luoma, J., & Guerrero, L. F. (2004). DBT, FAP, and ACT: How empirically oriented are the new behavior therapy technologies? *Behavior Therapy, 35*, 35–54.

Hook, J. N., Hook, J. P., & Hines, S. (2008). Reach out or act out: Long-term group therapy for sexual addiction. *Sexual Addiction and Compulsivity, 15*, 217–232.

Hook, J. N., Worthington, E. L., Jr., Hook, J. P., Miller, B. T., & Davis, D. E. (2011). Marriage matters: A description and initial examination of a church-based marital education program. *Pastoral Psychology, 60*, 869–875.

Hook, J. P., & Hook, J. N. (2010). The healing cycle: A Christian model for group therapy. *Journal of Psychology and Christianity, 29*, 308–316.

Hook, J. P., & Hook, J. N. (2015, September). The healing cycle: A process approach for leading small groups. Pre-conference workshop presented at the American Association of Christian Counselors World Conference, Nashville, September 23, 2015.

Jacobs, E. E., Masson, R. L., & Harvill, R. L. (2002). *Group counseling: Strategies and skills* (5th ed.). Pacific Grove, CA: Brooks/Cole.

Jones, E. (1963). *The life and work of Sigmund Freud.* Oxford: Doubleday.

Jones, E. E., & Nisbett, R. E. (1971). *The actor and the observer: Divergent perceptions of the causes of behavior.* Morristown, NJ: General Learning Press.

Joyce, A. S., Piper, W. E., Ogrodniczuk, J. S., & Klein, R. H. (2007). *Termination in psychotherapy: A psychodynamic model of processes and outcomes.* Washington, DC: American Psychological Association Press.

Keller, T. (2008). *The prodigal God: Recovering the heart of the Christian faith.* London: Penguin Books.

Kirchhoff, J., Strack, M., & Jager, U. (2009, July). Apologies: Depending on offence severity the composition of elements does matter. In F. Garoff

(Chair), *Preventing violent conflict: Psychological dimensions.* Symposium conducted at the 11th European Congress of Psychology, Oslo, Norway.

Lally, P., van Jaarsveld, C. H. M., Potts, H. W. W., & Wardle, J. (2010). How habits are formed: Modelling habit formation in the real world. *European Journal of Social Psychology, 40,* 998–1009.

Lewis, C. S. (1960). *The four loves.* London: Geoffrey Bles.

Luft, J. (1969). *Of human interaction.* Oxford: National Press.

Maslow, A. H. (1943). A theory of human motivation. *Psychological Review, 50,* 370–396.

McCullough, M. E., Worthington, E. L., Jr., & Rachal, K. C. (1997). Interpersonal forgiving in close relationships. *Journal of Personality and Social Psychology, 73,* 321–336.

McDonald, A., Beck, R., Allison, S., & Norsworthy, L. (2005). Attachment to God and parents: Testing the correspondence vs. compensation hypotheses. *Journal of Psychology and Christianity, 24,* 21–28.

Moon, G. (1997). *Homesick for Eden: A soul's journey to joy.* Ann Arbor, MI: Servant Publications.

Morris, F. R., & Morris, D. G. (1985). *The recognition and expression of feelings.* South Bend, IN: TACM.

Neimeyer, G. J. (1992). Personal constructs in career counseling and development. *Journal of Career Development, 18,* 163–174.

Ng, T. W. H., Sorensen, K. L., & Eby, L. T. (2006). Locus of control at work: A meta-analysis. *Journal of Organizational Behavior, 27,* 1057–1087.

Patterson, K., Grenny, J., McMillan, R., & Switzler, A. (2002). *Crucial conversations: Tools for talking when stakes are high.* New York: McGraw-Hill.

Peck, M. S. (1978). *The road less traveled: A new psychology of love, traditional values, and spiritual growth.* New York: Simon & Schuster.

Peck, M. S. (1987). *The different drum: Community making and peace.* New York: Simon & Schuster.

Prochaska, J. O., & DiClemente, C. C. (1986). Toward a comprehensive model of change. In W. R. Miller & N. Heather (Eds.), *Treating addictive behaviors: Processes of change* (pp. 3–27). New York: Springer.

Prochaska, J. O., Norcross, J. C., & DiClemente, C. C. (1994). *Changing for good: A revolutionary six-stage program for overcoming bad habits and moving your life positively forward.* New York: HarperCollins.

Rogers, C. R. (1957). The necessary and sufficient conditions of therapeutic personality change. *Journal of Consulting Psychology, 21,* 95–103.

Rotter, J. B. (1966). Generalized expectancies for internal versus external control of reinforcement. *Psychological Monographs: General and Applied, 80*, 1–28.

Sedikides, C., & Gregg, A. P. (2008). Self-enhancement: Food for thought. *Perspectives on Psychological Science, 3*, 102–116.

Skinner, B. F. (1953). *Science and human behavior.* New York: Macmillan.

Teyber, E. (1992). *Interpersonal process in psychotherapy: A guide for clinical training* (2nd ed.). Belmont, CA: Thomson Brooks/Cole Publishing Co.

Tschuschke, V., & Dies, R. R. (1994). Intensive analysis of therapeutic factors and outcome in long-term inpatient group. *International Journal of Group Psychotherapy, 44*, 185–208.

Tuckman, B. (1965). Developmental sequence in small groups. *Psychological Bulletin, 63*, 384–399.

Worthington, E. L., Jr. (1998). The Pyramid Model of Forgiveness: Some interdisciplinary speculations about unforgiveness and the promotion of forgiveness. In E. L. Worthington, Jr. (Ed.), *Dimensions of forgiveness: Psychological research and theological perspectives* (pp. 107–137). Philadelphia: Templeton Foundation Press.

Worthington, E. L., Jr. (2006). *Forgiveness and reconciliation: Theory and application.* New York: Routledge.

Yalom, I. D. (1970). *The theory and practice of group psychotherapy.* New York: Basic Books.

Yancey, P. (1997). *What's so amazing about grace?* Grand Rapids: Zondervan.

About the Authors

JAN PAUL HOOK (EdD) is a licensed clinical professional counselor (LCPC) in the state of Illinois. He does individual, marital, and group psychotherapy. He is in private practice in Arlington Heights, Illinois.

JOSHUA N. HOOK (PhD) is an associate professor of psychology at the University of North Texas, and he is a licensed clinical psychologist in the state of Texas. His research focuses on humility, religion/spirituality, and multicultural counseling. Josh also blogs regularly at www.JoshuaNHook.com.

DON E. DAVIS (PhD) is an associate professor of psychology at Georgia State University. His research and writing focus is on humility, forgiveness, and religion/spirituality.

Index